The

POIESIS POETRY GUIDE

for Colorado

Edited by
Catherine O'Neill Thorn

O'NEILL PUBLISHING

with support from

Columbine Poetry Society

Professional Book Center

This project is supported by funding from the Colorado Council on the Arts, a state agency funded by the Colorado General Assembly, and the National Endowment for the Arts, a federal agency.

Dedicated to the promotion of poetry
and the vision of a vital and cohesive community
of poets and poetry lovers
in the state of Colorado.

Poiesis (poy-áy-sis) is a Greek word meaning "creation" or "production."

The editor wishes to acknowledge the generous help of Bruce Kauffman (*Research Editor/Volunteer Coordinator*), Jennifer Cassidy, Tony Moffeit, Art Goodtimes, Carol Bauschke, Luba Haliki-Hoffman & Claudia Morell, without whom it would have been impossible to undertake the many tasks necessary to compile this information. And special thanks my "last-minute rescuers," Stephanie Saunders, Willie Domago, Gail Waldstein, Sandra McNew and Sally Ortiz.

Design	Catherine O'Neill Thorn
Cover Art/Photography	John Michael Thorn
Technical Support	Tim McMahon, Ruah Graphics
Printing	KIMCO

Please send all single-copy orders for this book $9.95 postpaid, and all editorial correspondence, including updates or corrections to: O'Neill Publishing, PO Box 53, Indian Hills, CO 80454 • E-mail: ONeillPub@aol.com. For information on the next edition of The Poiesis Poetry Guide for Colorado, visit us on the Web at www.sni.net/probook/poiesis.html.

Booksellers may order from Professional Book Center, PO Box 102650, Denver, CO 80250 • 800.848.6222 • probook@sni.net.

Library of Congress Cataloguing-in-Publishing data is available for this title.

ISBN 0-938075-7-3-X

Printed in the United States on acid free paper.

First edition.

CONTENTS

FOREWORD	*Lee Ballentine*	v
INTRODUCTION		1
ARTICLES		
The Spot—It's About Respect	*Carson Reed*	3
Going to Extremes	*Catherine O'Neill Thorn*	5
RESOURCE DIRECTORY		
Bookstores		9
Classes		15
Conferences/Festivals		17
Contacts/Organizations		19
Contests/Awards		27
Educational Facilities		33
Events		35
Performances		37
Publications		39
Radio		45
Readings		47
Venues		55
Workshops		59
Writers Groups		63
SERVICE DIRECTORY		65
POETS DIRECTORY		69

In 1991 I moved back to Denver after nearly 20 years away. As a poet—and sensing that there was a lively poetry scene—I looked for the newsletter, newspaper column, or broadsheet that would tell me where to go to hear poetry and who to buttonhole about reading my own work. San Francisco had *Poetry Flash*, New York had several events newsletters, but Denver seemed to have nothing comparable.

Before long—in a typical case of newcomer's zeal (though I grew up here)—I had compiled a list of 50 worthwhile local projects (available on request). I showed it to Renee Ruderman, a fine poet and well-loved teacher at Metropolitan State College. Upon seeing item #1, her eyes lit up. "I know someone who might be interested in making this happen," she said. This "someone" turned out to be Catherine O'Neill.

Discussions followed, and in the end, Catherine was interested, loved poetry enough, and was insufficiently cynical to understand that what was proposed was "impossible." She set about achieving the impossible, not alone of course—she had help throughout the spectrum of commitment—but it was Catherine who "made it happen"; she also gave POIESIS its name.

Apart from floating the idea and helping it get offshore, my main contribution was to write the "charter" for POIESIS, to ensure that it would remain informational in character, not critical or theoretical, and that it stay as far as possible from poetry politics. Denver, home of the "poetry wars" of the 60s and 70s, could not afford anything divisive in poetry—but that's another story. If you weren't around in this period, ask someone who was. There are tales to be told.

Catherine and her cohorts built POIESIS up to about 5,000 circulation and had many successes, but in the end she could not carry POIESIS and make a life too. When no one else stepped up to shoulder the responsibility, POIESIS, as a newsletter, ceased to exist.

But along the way Catherine had become the "expert" on Colorado poetry—the contact for local and national media. And now POIESIS has risen from the ashes as a book, a web site, and who knows what else may come. I urge you, if you care about poetry in Colorado, take note of this book and ask others to do the same. Many of you are already "making things happen" in poetry—and the synergy of connection POIESIS makes possible can only lead to more, and more vital, poetry action of many, many kinds.

Lee Ballentine

Often over the last several years as I have sought to promote poetry in Colorado, I have been asked by well-meaning—and sometimes even irate *("You call that poetry?")*—individuals to define poetry. It is like being asked to define God. Not only am I limited by my own individual consciousness, but I also am limited by circumscribed and often inadequately applied tools of communication. The funnel becomes even narrower.

To attempt to offer my individual conception of an infinite power with limited means seems futile. And yet we do it all the time. Because that's what poetry does. It is, in fact, one of the purposes of art: to help define the unimaginable, as well as the commonality of our existence, to create order out of chaos, to lend form to inarticulated emotion. To communicate. Are we then to assume we are at liberty to judge that communication based on whether or not it fits our own personal definition? Rather, true communication extends beyond the self and must encompass the whole.

Diversity is a concept only recently touted, albeit politically, as the key to unity. Just as it is not enough to have one poet, it is not enough to have one definition of poetry. There are some who are amazingly brilliant in their perceptions, gifted in communication, and who have the skills necessary to garner an audience. But then there are others who, although gifted with their own unique perceptions, have not learned the skills of the language, nor have found their voice. Many poets have been silenced either by their own feelings of inadequacy or by various other more overt means, such as racism, sexism, poverty, religion or politics. Each individual voice is vital, but only when joined to the chorus of other voices. In our limited perceptions and our limited use of the language, we can only express a trickle of the truth, however brilliant or enlightening that trickle may be. It is still only a glimmer of the wide glory that exists outside our finite imaginations. Only when our voices are joined can we catch a glimpse of who we are, what we are called to be, the world outside our encasement of flesh and its furious demands.

POIESIS was designed to aid in that joining. In 1992, myself and a small group of students caught the vision of a local publisher, Lee Ballentine, and started a poetry newsletter and calendar of events for the state of Colorado. In the four years POIESIS was published, more than 100,000 copies of the newsletter were distributed—most in Colorado, but also across the nation and to several other countries. Attendance at poetry events soared, new groups flourished and media attention increased as poets were better able to network and support each other, and the public became more aware of the power and relevance of poetry. As funding for the arts has decreased nationally, the results have been discouraging. Despite the fact that poetry promotes all that our leaders endorse: healing, community, diversity and change, poetry has not received the attention or the funding it needs to thrive as an effective vehicle for personal and social development. Thanks to the vision of those who continue to support the arts: members of the Colorado Council on the Arts, the Columbine Poetry Society and yourself, we can provide vital information to help the poets and poetry lovers in the state of Colorado continue to access their resources and combine their talents.

Despite our best efforts, there are bound to be organizations and services we missed, changes of which we were not informed, as well as the inadvertent error. For these we apologize and ask that you inform us of necessary changes needing to be made for any subsequent publications.

It is my hope that you will use this book to explore the many and diverse poetry resources throughout our state, that you will make vital connections with other poets in order to promote the development of a united community of those who respect the power of poetry, and that you will encourage others to discover the joy and benefit of supporting poetry events in Colorado.

Catherine O'Neill Thorn

The Spot

It's All About Respect

Carson Reed

An example of the "Youth Art" that decorates many of the walls at The Spot.

Barely noticeable in the desolate DMZ between Coors Field and Curtis Park there is an oasis for music, poetry and art. Its doors closed against the daylight world, the old warehouse (the former Paramount Pictures film archive and screening room at 21st and Stout) comes alive at five, the action building as the sun sets behind the mountains west of Denver.

On a recent hot, hot, hot afternoon, there was already a buzz of early activity around the place. A dozen or so kids — around here everyone seems to refer to themselves as "youth" are *hard at work* — honing their skills as writers, musicians, artists, poets, dancers.

No, this isn't the alternative school. This is The Spot, and even though it is still a dream that is very much under construction, it takes very little imagination to see that this is gonna be, well, *pretty dope.*

Even in its unfinished state, this is certainly close to a B-Boy's dream of what his bedroom might look like in a perfect world: a break dance floor replete with mirrored walls for critical self-inspection, walls fresh (as in *blank*) waiting for graffiti which will likewise be fresh (as in *cool*).

But this also promises to be some kind of techno-paradise for the terminally creative. There's a full recording studio nearly completed, a photo lab under construction, and upstairs a slew of computers that are used to generate The Spot's very fine lit-zine, *Inner 303* — and sometimes, you know, for a couple games of *Doom.*

Looking to provide a safe and interesting evening environment for the young men and women living in Denver's inner city, Spot Director Dave DeForest-Stalls has spent the last couple of years unraveling the puzzle of what he could possibly offer more interesting than the streets themselves. What started out in his mind as a non-profit coffeehouse has become (kind of by accident I think) — a *creative arts center,* attracting the attention of some of the shining stars of Denver's dynamic youth subculture. There is one rule at The Spot: Respect.

"Everything leads off from that," DeForest-Stalls says. And it's something you can see. Stylized street attitude abounds, but the kids are here to learn *from each other* how to dance, write, D.J., whatever, and the less experienced allow the experienced their modicum of respect — *props.* And it cuts both ways. The staff here, starting with DeForest-Stalls, are learning from the young people he calls "my customers."

The staff, in fact, are mostly creative types themselves, not here to teach or counsel so much as to fill in the gaps — to provide the expertise, direction and support needed to help turn artistic impulses into art. Music Director Devin "Ivory" West has spliced together a respectable sound studio, and kids hunch over the keyboards and mixing boards every evening, working on their mixes, recording hip-hip tunes in the sound booth, many of them preparing material for a CD that The Spot hopes to release this Fall.

George, one of the "mostly creative" staff members.

Likewise, Peggy DeForest-Stalls (yup, Dave's wife) presides over *Inner 303* less as an editor and more as a facilitator, coach and cheering section. Accepted work goes unedited, a reflection of *Inner 303*'s stated manifesto that its intent is to "listen, illuminate and respect, not to critique or judge."

Non-fiction offerings dominate: sometimes confrontational ("Will the Real Criminals Stand Up?" Spring '97), sometimes political ("Let's Keep the Paz," Spring '97) sometimes heartbreaking ("Clint R. Martinez," summer '97), they are all starkly earnest; the expressions of a generation that is thinking hard and long about the world they are inheriting.

Poetry sublimates: In its unedited state, the best work of *Inner 303* is as fresh and muscular as any poetry you will encounter anywhere, words from the heart. What makes it striking is the range of experience, much of it horrific, that makes young voices sound old. But what makes it also remarkable is the optimism implicit in the writing of it — the collective courage of kids overcoming long odds.

Art reiterates: Images by a generation, for a generation, assert the richness of the culture they are creating more forcefully than words ever could — remarkable airbrush fantasies, pencil drawings of the beautiful and the grotesque, photography that captures the most striking faces and moments.

"Adults are always trying to tell kids what culture is, what art is," Deforest-Stalls says. "Trying to teach them that without *even looking* at *their* art, *their* culture — that's the ultimate disrespect."

Going to Extremes

Poetry that screams for attention

Catherine O'Neill Thorn

I have always been terrified of teenagers. It started when *I* was a teenager — and nothing in my 20-odd years of experience has since given me good cause to rescind that fear. So it always seems a bit odd, even to me, when I find myself in front of 21 teenage boys — all of whom have been labeled either criminals, addicts or perpetrators — teaching poetry.

The Going to Extremes poetry therapy program began as an experiment. Although I believe in the healing power of poetry, I wasn't sure of my reception. In fact, I dreaded the imagined apathy and (God forbid!) outright animosity the presentation might generate. And yet, the typical attitude of the boys to the poets I bring into the program and the poetry generated from the workshops has always been one of respect and cooperation. I am still amazed and moved by the overwhelming positive response all these different boys passing through the program have had to poetry. I may not have changed my opinion about teenagers, but I have grown to care for them regardless.

Despite my initial apprehension, I have found myself in front of these boys more and more often. I conduct poetry readings and workshops with them, take them to poetry readings in town, and read children's books to them once a week. Because of the opportunities I have been given to interact with these young men, I've discovered something very significant to me: these violent adolescents are nevertheless children — children who have equated childhood with abuse and sorrow; children who are afraid to be young and vulnerable in a vicious world; children who *must* be given a chance to heal. That is why I read children's books to them and teach them poetry. In this small way, I attempt to give them back not only a taste of childhood but an avenue in which they can express some vulnerability.

One of the young men in my poetry therapy sessions, 13-year-old Tony, would come to each session and sit quietly without participating. He wore a black hooded sweatshirt, with the hood up, and would fold himself into the corner, occasionally peering out of the opening in his hood with apprehension. He was a sexual perpetrator — and had been a victim of sexual abuse from an even younger age. After the first three weeks, I asked him to please write me one small poem. He was reluctant, and as I cajoled him, one of the older boys reprimanded me: "You said none of us has to participate, if we don't want to."

He was right, of course, but I have noticed that with some young men, their reluctance is based purely on fear of rejection. I wanted to assure Tony that his poetry would be respected. That his voice would be heard.

At the end of the program, Tony shyly approached me with the following poem:

ISOLATION

I sit in the corner
not knowing what to do
not wanting to talk
but people want me to
wanting to cry
not able to
not knowing why
God! I want to cry

Despite my assurance that his poem was valuable and meaningful, Tony did not participate again for another couple of months. During one session, the exercise was for the boys to write about something they could offer the world. I asked Tony if he would write another poem for me. He looked scared and quickly shook his head, no. "Don't you have something you could give to the world, Tony?" I asked him. Again, he shook his head, no, but also added, "I don't know." — an opening, if ever I heard one.

"Hasn't anyone ever told you that you have a special gift?" I persisted.

"No," he replied.

"Has anyone ever said 'thank you' for something you did?" I tried again.

"No," he repeated.

"That's not true, Tony." I said. "One time I asked you to write a poem for me, when you didn't want to. And you wrote me a lovely poem. That tells me you have a big, generous heart. Doesn't the world need that, more than anything?"

I saw his eyes light up, and a brief smile flickered across his face.

"I guess."

"Well," I continued, "Assuming you were to give your heart, would you hold it close to you, as if afraid?"

"No!" he said, emphatically. I was surprised.

"How would you give it?" I asked.

He stretched his arms out in front of him. "Like this." He looked happy.

"Why don't you write a poem for me about how that would feel, to give your heart away? And how you would want someone to take it from you."

He looked serious and nodded his head once.

When he handed me the poem a short while later on a torn piece of notebook paper, he told me he didn't want to read it out loud. When I asked if I could read it to the group for him, he nodded.

I stood at the microphone and asked the rest of the group to listen to

Tony's poem.

IF I WAS GOING TO GIVE MY HEART

If I was going to give my heart
I would put it out into an open space
Whoever wants it can take it
Take as much as you like
I have a lot to give
But please be gentle
My heart is fragile
Don't throw it in my face
It would break
My heart is already scarred
I don't want another
Be gentle, I care
—Even if you don't
I care
Please
Take my love

When I finished reading there was an emotional silence. Then the boys did something I had never seen before. After the applause, several of them got up and gave Tony a hug. All responded with words of respect and admiration. From what I could tell, Tony's poem expressed what many of these boys feel: a desire to be recognized; to be held and loved; to give love.

How many of us want to be known for more than just our behavior? How many of us have engaged in destructive or foolish behavior due to an ignorance about our value and/or potential? In giving these boys an opportunity to use language to express what is more true than their behavior, we also can take a moment to listen with our own hearts, instead of with our fear.

Yes, these boys are scary ... because they do scary things to themselves and others. They may be wounded children, but they certainly aren't innocent victims. In fact, the situation is more complex than most of us are willing to acknowledge or address. But I, like the staff of Lost and Found Inc., believe in redemption. Most of these boys are more afraid of themselves than we are of them. Most of them would love to be given the chance to love — and a sanctuary in which to do it.

Poetry is one place of shelter. Although the language of metaphor reveals more than we as writers are aware, revelation is something we all crave: the chance to be known and heard. Now all that is needed is someone to listen. And someone to care.

** If you would like to support the program in any ways (books, funds, writing materials, etc.), please contact Catherine O'Neill Thorn, PO Box 53, Indian Hills, CO 80454 • 303.697.1317 • 303.697.9799 (FAX) • ONeillPub@aol.com*

BOULDER

Jim, Manager
Aion Bookshop
303.443.5763
1235 Pennsylvania Ave.
Boulder CO 80302
Aionbook@interloc.com

Provides extensive poetry selection, including publications by local poets; hosts Naropa Institute student readings. Call for more information.

Tom Peters, Poet/Proprietor
Beat Book Shop
303.444.7111
303.444.5322 (FAX)
1713 Pearl Street
Boulder CO 80302

Extensive selection of poetry. Open 1-7 p.m. Sun. through Tues.; 12-9 p.m. Wed. through Sat. Tom Peters hosts weekly readings at Penny Lane Coffeehouse (see listing under Readings).

Lisa Gesner, Manager
Boulder Book Store
303.447.2074
303.447.9539 (FAX)
1107 Pearl St.
Boulder CO 80302
BoulderBk@aol.com
www.boulderbookstore.com

Poetry section features a Beat selection that highlights Naropa poets. Boulder Book Store has an ongoing commitment to support local poets and local small presses. Sponsors annual April Poetry Month celebration (poetry readings, give-aways, contest), and the Annual Small Press Reading in early summer. Presents over 100 author events per year & creative writing workshops on an ongoing basis.

Louise Knapp
Word is Out Women's Bookstore
303.449.1415
1713 15th St.
Boulder CO 80302

Sporadic readings. Call for more information.

COLORADO SPRINGS

Chris Tauscher, Contact
Barnes & Noble Bookstore
719.637.8282
719.637.8388 (FAX)
795 Citadel Dr. East
Colorado Springs CO 80909

Hosts readings, book signings and amateur poetry night. Hours: 9 a.m.-11 p.m., seven days a week.

Bill Porter
Bijou Street Bookfinders
719.578.5044
17 E. Bijou
Colorado Springs CO 80905

Used books; out-of-print search.

Jim Ciletti, Contact
La Dolce Vita
719.632.1369
333 N. Tejon
Colorado Springs CO 80903

Bookstore/Coffeehouse: primarily used books, large literary/poetry sections. Performances & Workshops vary, as do groups, events, styles, dates and times.

Richard Skorman, Owner
Poor Richard's Restaurant/Bookstore
719.578.0012
719.578.0323 (FAX)
320 N. Tejon
Colorado Springs CO 80903

The bookstore offers a poetry section & hosts book signings. Open Sun.-Thurs. 10 a.m. to 8 p.m. & Fri./Sat. 9:30 a.m. to 9 p.m. The restaurant/coffeehouse presents open readings & "Bare Knuckle Poetry" every third Tues. of the month from 7-10 p.m.

DENVER

Celia, Contact
Cultural Legacy
303.964.9049
3633 West 32nd Ave.
Denver CO 80211

Latino bookstore; hosts readings.

Robert Bredeck, Owner
Gibson's Bookstore
303.620.0034
1404 Larimer St.
Denver CO 80202

New and used books, as well as Auraria textbooks (new and used); features national, international and local poetry selections & framed poetry displays; also sells stationary and paper products.

The Book Garden
303.399.2004
303.399.6167 (FAX)
2625 E. 12th Ave.
Denver CO 80206

Extensive women's poetry selection.

Joyce Meskis, Owner
Jackie St. Joan, Host
Tattered Cover LoDo
Second Monday Poetry Series
303.436.1070
800.833.9327 (Toll Free)
303.322.1965 x 7446 (Events)
1536 Wynkoop St.
Denver CO 80202
newslttr@tatteredcover.com

Our Poetry Series and our exceptional poetry selection invite you to indulge yourself in the pure intensity of poetry. Each month we offer readings by local, regional, and national or international poets. The Second Monday Poetry Series is on the second Monday of the month and takes place in the LoDo store at 7:30 p.m. Please join us. To receive our Poetry Series flyer, call 322.1965 ext. 2700 or E-mail: newslttr@tatteredcover.com.

Lois Harvey
West Side Books
303.561.0035
303.480.5193 (FAX)
3600 West 32nd Ave., Suite C
Denver CO 80211
cellebooklh@aol.com

Writers workshop meets on Sundays. Must call, classes fill quickly. Will be hosting readings in the future (just relocated).

ESTES PARK

Dan & Louise Smith, Owners
Fine Old Books
970.586.6384
120 E. Riverside
PO Box 3928
Estes Park CO 80517

Antique books. 10 percent discount offered to those who mention this listing.

FORT COLLINS

Tom Rowland, Owner
Happenstance
970.493.1668
136 W. Mountain Ave.
Ft. Collins CO 80524

Offers a 10 percent discount to published poets and an extensive poetry selection. Owner intends to sponsor readings at the store as space allows.

Mark LaFrambois
Stone Lion Bookstore
970.493.0030
107 N. College Ave.
Ft. Collins CO 80524
stonelionbook.com

Hosts authors on tour (readings and booksignings); extensive poetry selection; hosts occasional readings. Hosts the annual fall reading, "Writer's Harvest." Proceeds go to the Larimer County food bank.

GREELEY

Hans Knoop, Owner
Prairie Reader
970.392.1008
919 16th St.
Greeley CO 80631
praireader@ctos.com

Offers 10 percent discount on books bought by poets who mention this listing.

LOVELAND

Michelle Lamothe & John Calhoun, Owners
Book Rack of Loveland
970.667.0118
138 E. 29th St. (Palmer Gardens)
Loveland CO 80538
lamothe1@aol.com

Offers a 10 percent discount on books to poets (mention this listing).

NORWOOD

Frances Baer, Director
Bear Paw Books & Gifts
970.327.4266
1611 Grand Ave.
Norwood CO 81423

Hosts occasional poetry readings.

PUEBLO

Elaine Brown, Contact
Barnes & Noble Bookstore
719.542.0698
719.542.0371 (FAX)
4300 N. Freeway
Pueblo CO 81008

Open readings & occasional guest readers on first Fri. each month: 7-8:30 p.m.

Nancy Dee, Contact
Books By the Bridge
719.542.5943
719.544.6250
310 S. Victoria Ave., Suite B
Pueblo CO 81002

General, independent bookstore sponsors poetry readings and book signings each Saturday, and a monthly book discussion group.

Amy Matthew, Contact
Hastings Books, Music & Video
719.564.9330
719.564.9254 (FAX)
1805 S. Pueblo Blvd.
Pueblo CO 81005

Hosts book signings, poetry readings and music performances. Hours: 10 a.m.-11 p.m., seven days a week.

TELLURIDE

Edi Katz, Owner
Between the Covers Bookstore
970.728.4504
224 W. Colorado Ave.
PO Box 1439
Telluride CO 81435

Hosts occasional poetry readings and booksignings.

Gina, Director
Bookworks
970.728.0770
191 S. Pine St.
Telluride CO 81435

Hosts occasional poetry readings and booksignings.

WINDSOR

Renée Johnson & Jackie Wiggins, Owners
Books/N/Things
970.686.0583
414A Main St.
Windsor CO 80550

Hosts featured readings and booksignings on the second and fourth Sat. of every month.

DENVER

Mike Sayers, Contact
Corona Presbyterian Church
303.832.2297
1205 E. 8th
Denver CO
CorPresChu@aol.com

Classes and coffeehouse third Friday of each month, except Dec.

Michael J. Henry & Andrea Dupree
Lighthouse Writers, Inc.
303.297.1185
2000 Arapahoe St. Suite 205
Denver CO 80205
AEDupree@aol.com

Lighthouse Writers originated in Boston and is dedicated to broadening access to serious writing classes and workshops to all poets/writers in Colorado. We love literature, teaching, and writing, and have taught writing for several years at Emerson College and Northeastern University. Although we both completed MFA programs to fulfill our needs for structure, support, and guidance, we feel that high-quality alternatives must be available to writers who have full lives and cannot afford the luxury of going to such full-time programs.

Classes: On-going poetry, fiction and creative writing classes, held in Bayly Loft space at 20th & Arapahoe (upper Larimer), Instructors are poet Michael Henry, MFA, and fiction writer Andrea Dupree, MFA. Not accredited.

ASPEN

Jeannie, Director
Julie Comins, Contact
Aspen Writers' Foundation
970.925.3122
800.925.2526
303.970.5700 (FAX)
320 W. Main
PO Box 7726
Aspen CO 81612-7726
Aspenwrite@aol.com

The annual Aspen Writers' Conference, one of the oldest and most well-respected literary programs in the country, is held in June of each year. Program includes workshops in Poetry, Fiction, Memoir Writing, Children's Literature and offers readings, industry talks, craft lectures and networking opportunities. Faculty members are selected for their outstanding reputations as teachers as well as writers, and talented writers at all levels of experience are welcome. The program presents morning workshops, afternoon lectures and evening readings, interspersed with guest speakers, special events and free time. Enrollment is limited; material must be submitted to gain acceptance into the program (Poets: up to eight pages; Fiction, Non-Fiction & Children's Literature: up to 20 pages). Audit passes and tickets to individual events also are available.

DENVER AREA

Anita Jepson-Gilbert
303.465.0883
Margaret Walther
303.755.3638
Columbine Poetry Society
Poets of the Foothills Art Center
10751 Routt St.
Broomfield CO 80021
wagil@aol.com

Columbine Poets is the official state poetry society for Colorado, affiliated with the National Federation of State Poetry Societies. Membership is open to any resident of Colorado interested in poetry. State membership dues of $8 also entitle membership in the National Federation. There currently are two chapters in Colorado: the Foothills chapter and the Evergreen chapter. The Annual Foothills Poets Fest is held each June with workshops and featured readings (call Anita Jepson-Gilbert for more information).

Sandy Whelchel, Executive Director
National Writer's Association
303.751.7844
303.751.8593 (FAX)
1450 S. Havana St., Suite 424
Aurora CO 80012

A service organization for writers at all levels and in all disciplines. Many of our 3,000 members are poets as well as writers in other genres. NWA memberships are $65 for Regular, $85 for Professional and $35 for students with ID. NWA holds a yearly national Summer Conference in the Denver area on the second weekend in June. Authorities in all disciplines, including nationally-known poets give workshops on various subjects relating to poetry. Speakers change yearly.

STEAMBOAT SPRINGS

Harriet Freiberger, Director
970.879.8079
970.879.9062 (FAX)
Steamboat Springs Writers Group
PO Box 774284
Steamboat Springs CO 80477
freiberger@compuserve.com

Steamboat Springs Writers Group, sponsored by the Steamboat Springs Arts Council, meets weekly to discuss and critique poetry, fiction and non-fiction. Everyone is welcome. Conferences, held over the last sixteen years, emphasize small seminar format and feature a variety of instructors. Registration is limited for the annual mid-July event.

TELLURIDE

Art Goodtimes, Director
Telluride Writers Guild
970.327.4775
Box 1008
Telluride CO 81435

Talking Gourds Annual Poetry Festival, second weekend in July. Opening with a performance in Telluride Thurs. night. Ah Haa School for the Arts sponsors a three-day workshop: Fri.-Sun. at the Faraway Ranch on Wilson Mesa.

BOULDER

Linda Woods
Boulder Writers' Alliance
303.530.9010
PO Box 18342
Boulder CO 80308-1342
Web Site: www.bwa.org

The Boulder Writers Alliance (BWA) is a nonprofit organization of communications professionals. Goals: to help members find work and to increase our marketable skills. BWA's diverse membership includes specialists in technical writing and editing, copywriting, corporate communications, journalism, fiction and nonfiction writing, online help, World Wide Web design, desktop publishing and graphic arts. The group meets monthly and sponsors a variety of seminars & workshops.

Jim Cohn, Contact
Museum of American Poetics
303.444.4490
jimcohn@ecentral.com

The Museum of American Poetics (MAP) is the sponsor of "Poets on Poets," an interactive lecture series that will feature MAP curator-poets exploring the life & work of six Americans whose poetry has changed the way we look at the contemporary poem, including talks, writings, readings and performances of various US poets. Submissions for exhibits are welcome for MAP, the first internationally oriented center dedicated to the preservation and exhibition of American poetry and its influences.

Laurie Kay Olson, Contact
Poetry Society of Colorado, Inc.
303.449.1325
2635 Mapleton #10
Boulder CO 80304

General meetings are held quarterly on the third Sun. of Oct. (at the Trinity Methodist Church in Denver), Dec., Feb. and April (at the Glendale Community Center) at 1:30 p.m. Contest results and guest speakers will be announced beforehand. Annual awards are presented on the first Sat. in June at noon at the Wyndham Gardens, 1475 S. Colorado Blvd.

Dr. James Hutchinson
Rocky Mountain Writer's Guild
Live Poets' Society
303.444.4100
837 15th St.
Boulder CO 80302

Organization meets monthly; must be selected to be in the society. Poetry society readings and criticism held the second Fri. of every month, 7-10 p.m.

Tom Peters, Contact
"So, You're A Poet Productions"
Penny Lane Coffeehouse
303.443.9516
1713 Pearl St.
Boulder CO 80302

Presents a weekly reading on Mon. at Penny Lane Coffeehouse, 18th & Pearl, Boulder. Sept.1 through May 30: 8-11 p.m.; June/July/Aug.: 9 p.m.-midnight.

Jerrie Hurd, Editor
Women Writing the West
303.444.9139 (Phone & FAX)
PO Box 12
Boulder CO 80306
JerrieHurd@aol.com
Web Site: www.sni.net/www-writers

A marketing and networking organization similar to Sister in Crime, which helps women mystery writers draw attention to their work. In our case, we publish a newsletter and catalog of writers' works and take tables at Booksellers Conferences among other things, to promote all writing about the women's West, including poetry. Some members had work included in the new anthology, LEANING INTO THE WIND, and have given performances at Cowboy Poetry Festivals.

COLORADO SPRINGS

Robert Dassanowsky, President
Teresa Jillson: Vice President
Northern Colorado Representative: Robert Carl Cohen
PEN Colorado: A regional chapter of PEN USA/West (Los Angeles)
719.262.3562
719.262.3146 (FAX)
Robert Dassanowsky: Pres. PEN Colorado
c/o Dept. of Languages and Cultures
University of Colorado
1420 Austin Bluffs
Colorado Springs CO 80933
e-mail: rvondass@mail.uccs.edu
Web Site: http://www.uccs.edu/~rvondass/pen.html

Founded in 1994, PEN Colorado is the Rocky Mountain regional chapter of PEN USA/West, one of two PEN Centers in the U.S., and the fourth largest center of Int'l. PEN (headquarters in London) in the world. Its mission is to promote a vital literary community in the western U.S., to arouse and maintain interest in the written word, and to advance freedom of expression throughout the world. PEN Colorado focuses on the realities and concerns of the writers, poets, critics, historians, journalists, screenwriters, playwrights, translators and editors in the Colo. and Wyo. area. Membership is by application to all those, regardless of nationality, race, gender or religion, who have demonstrated work of substantial literary value — book publication, productions, editorship, special contributions to the literary community. Membership includes invitations to PEN events and workshops; listing in the PEN Member Directory; subscription to PEN's magazine, ***Center;*** involvement in PEN's Freedom-to Write activities; participation on PEN Committees; opportunity to attend international PEN Congresses.

Elizabeth Smith: 719.636.1257
Lois Hayna: 719.599.0502
John Thelin: 719.578.5909
Poetry West
P.O. Box 2143
Colorado Springs CO 80901

Poetry West is a nonprofit organization bringing poetry workshops and readings to the Pikes Peak region. All are free and open to the public, and usually held on the first Fri. and/or Sat. of each month. Locations and poet speakers vary. Poetry West welcomes new members. Dues are $25/year. Poetry West also provides occasional workshops and/or readings for various groups, including senior citizens, schools, prisons and detention centers. ***the eleventh MUSE*** accepts submissions of three to five poems, any style (see entry under PUBLICATIONS).

DENVER AREA

Sue Gibbons, Director
The Christian Fine Arts Association
303.680.5519 (Phone & FAX)
P.O. Box 22155
Denver CO 80222
73311,466@compuserve.com

A ministry for the purpose of glorifying God and His Works through creative expression in the fine arts. Our organization's goal is to establish an environment where Christian artists can have fellowship, develop spiritually as well as professionally, and present work that is uplifting and challenging. Membership: Individual $30; Family $40; Seniors $25; Students $25; Associate $25.

Kimberly Taylor, Executive Director
Megan Maguire, Contact
303.839.8323
Colorado Center for the Book
303.866.6976
303.866.6940 (FAX)
2123 Downing St.
Denver CO 80205

The Colorado Center for the Book (CCFTB) envisions a state where all people are literate and there is a community focus on the joy of reading and support of books and the book arts. CCFTB takes an active role in promoting reading and writing as a value in Colorado. We produce highly visible promotional activities and form partnerships with organizations sharing similar goals. The Colorado Center for the Book embraces Colorado poetry in a variety of ways:

- The Rocky Mountain Book Festival is an annual event that features published poets in workshops, panel discussions and readings.
- The Colorado Center for the Book also organizes the selection of the Colorado Poet Laureate—chosen for a four-year term.
- The Colorado Book Awards are held annually by the CCFTB. Any author/poet living in Colorado with a book published in a given year is eligible.

The Center for the Book holds a variety of other events throughout the year for Colorado authors and poets. If you are interested in participating, call Megan Maguire (above).

Daniel Salazar, Associate Director
Colorado Council on the Arts
303.894.2619
303.894.2615 (FAX)
800.291.ARTS (Toll Free)
750 Pennsylvania Street
Denver CO 80203-3699
daniel.salazar@ossinc.net

The Colorado Council on the Arts presents the following opportunities for artists:

- The Artist Fellowship Awards: an annual fellowship award that provides recognition and funding support to outstanding Colorado artists in performing arts, media arts, visual arts and literature (including poetry, fiction/nonfiction and playwriting/screenwriting) on a rotating cycle. Contact Daniel Salazar, Associate Director of the CCA, for more information.
- Art in Public Places Program: 1 percent laws have taken root and are blossoming throughout the nation. Contact Roberta Kaserman, Director of CCA's Art in Public Places Program, for more information.
- Artists-in-Residence Program: Young Audiences manages CCA's arts education programs. CCA urgently seeks artists from Greater Colorado to participate. Call Patty Ortiz, Program Director of Young Audiences, Inc., for more information.

Ashley Kasprzak, Contact
Colorado Endowment for the Humanities
303.573.7733
303.573.7722 (FAX)
1623 Blake St.
Denver CO 80202

Distributes grants to nonprofit organizations that support the humanities. Offers educational events and a potential funding source for public programs. Presents an author luncheon yearly to correspond with the Rocky Mountain Book Festival. Call for more information.

Anita Jepson-Gilbert: 303.465.0883
Margaret Walther: 303.755.3638
Columbine Poetry Society
Poets of the Foothills Art Center
10751 Routt St.
Broomfield CO 80021
wagil@aol.com

Columbine Poets is the official state poetry society for Colorado, affiliated with the National Federation of State Poetry Societies. Membership is open to any resident of Colorado. State membership dues of $8 entitle membership in the National Federation, as well. Currently, there are two chapters in Colorado: the Foothills chapter and the Evergreen chapter. Poetry writing classes offered each Saturday, 10am-12 noon (call for details). The Annual Foothills Poets Fest is held each June with workshops and featured readings (call Anita Jepson-Gilbert). Critiquing workshops are every 3rd Sunday at 1:30 pm (call Margaret Walther).

Peggy R. Leppek, Editor
Denver Word Affiliate
303.831.7452
P.O. Box 2913
Denver CO 80201-2913

Denver Word Affiliate is designed to create new opportunities and projects for writers and audiences, to unite a community of wordists, to recruit an inclusive membership in the Denver and Front Range community, to found an organization of wordists, to form a collective effort, to be respectful of all work, to encourage participants to promote poetic expression and diversity. DWA also publishes a bi-monthly poetry newsletter called ***Denver Word*** (premiere issue Aug. '97). Membership is $15 (newsletter only); $35 Individual; $100 Group/Patron.

Marge Tanaiwaki, Contact
Making Waves: Asians in Action
303.333.2130
303.592.1510 (FAX)
6100 E. Severn Pl.
Denver CO 80220

Readers theater that occasionally incorporates poetry.

Sandy Whelchel, Executive Director
National Writer's Association
303.751.7844
303.751.8593 (FAX)
1450 S. Havana St., Suite 424
Aurora CO 80012

A service organization for writers at all levels and in all disciplines. Many of our 3,000 members are poets as well as writers in other areas. Membership includes bi-monthly magazine, ***Authorship,*** as well as low-cost critiques, edits, marketing suggestions, contract reading and information on rights and copyrights. The Nov./ Dec. issue of each ***Authorship*** is devoted to poetry: subscription $20 per year. Memberships: $65 for Regular; $85 for Professional; and $35 for students with ID. NWA Poetry Contest runs from July 1 to October 1 yearly (see entry under Contests/Awards). NWA holds a yearly national Summer Conference in the Denver area on the second weekend in June (see entry under Conferences/Festivals).

Roseanna Frechette, Contact
The Power of Poetic Voice
Girls Inc. of Metro Denver
303.837.8425
303.893.4363
3444 W. Colfax Ave.
Denver CO

A 10-week after school program for the members of Girls Incorporated of Metro Denver, inner city club for youth. This program recently won an Outstanding Program Award from Girls Incorporated national headquarters in New York. The class meets weekly, and is designed and facilitated by Roseanna Frechette (call for exact time and club membership information). The program runs seasonally and culminates in a public library reading of poems by the girls who wrote them.

Kay Adams, Contact
303.421.2298
Paula Hagar, Contact (Poetry Peer Circle)
303.329.0943
Whole Body Health
198 Union Blvd. #210
Lakewood CO 80228
KayAdams@aol.com.

Poetry Peer Circle, second Sun. of each month from 1:30-4:30 p.m. All are welcome to create and share poetry in a warm, non-judgmental, non-critical group setting. No experience or background needed. Near 6th & Simms in Lakewood.

Associated with the National Association for Poetry Therapy, a multidisciplinary professional organization for helping professionals, educators, poets, writers. Educational, networking and credentialing opportunities in developmental and/or clinical poetry therapy. Contact Alicia Seeger, NAPT, PO Box 551, Port Washington NY 11050 or www.poetrytherapy.org.

EVERGREEN

Carolyn Wangaard, Contact
303.674.5023
Evergreen Poets & Writers
PO Box 714
Evergreen CO 80437

Evergreen Poets & Writers, affiliated with the Columbine Poetry Society, publishes ***Buffalo Bones,*** a nonprofit Colorado publication of poetry and prose, and sponsors poetry readings at the Evergreen Lake House.

LOVELAND

Tom Katsimpalis, Curator of Interpretation
Loveland Museum and Gallery
970.962.2410
970.962.2910
5th & Lincoln
Loveland CO 80537

Presents a poetry series with featured readers in the fall and spring.

NUCLA

Ruth Sampson, Director
West End Literary Guild
970.864.2176
838 Main St.
Nucla CO 81424

Occasional gatherings for writers and poets.

PUEBLO

Tony Moffeit, Poet-in-Residence; Dept. Chair of Library
University of Southern Colorado
719.549.2751
719.549.2738 (FAX)
2200 Bonforte Blvd.
Pueblo CO 81001
moffeit@uscolo.edu

Directs poetry writing workshops. Organizes a celebration for Buzzard Day, each March 15th. Provides performances with musicians.

TELLURIDE

Robin Machado, Director
Wilkinson Library
970.728.6613
134 S. Spruce St.
Telluride CO 81435

PROJECTS: Gourd Circle Reading Series: hosts site for TWG's monthly readings

WRITERS IN THE SKY: local literary sojourn including poet Simon Ortiz. Oct. 25, 1997. Director: Ann Kennedy

POETS IN PERSON: four week program featuring work of Allen Ginsburg, Sharon Olds, Gary Soto, and Rita Dove in October; from 7-9 p.m. Director: Rosemerry Wahtola Trommer. Call for specific dates.

NORTHERN COLORADO/WYOMING

Steven Smith, Contact
307.635.2359
Serendipity Poets
415 West 28th St.
Cheyenne WY 82001
ChySerendp@aol.com

Serendipity Poets provides readings, community projects, contacts, events, performances and classes for northern Colorado and Wyoming poets at the Coffee Cup Gallery in Cheyenne (307.638.2077).

BOULDER

John Kellow, Literary Arts Editor
Boulder Planet
303.444.5761
303.415.1210 (FAX)
2028 14th St.
Boulder CO 80302

The Boulder Planet is a free weekly periodical with a literary arts section. Poetry is published twice monthly. The Boulder Planet also sponsors an Annual Poetry and Prose Contest. Call for more information.

Richard Wilmarth, Owner
Dead Metaphor Press
303.939.0268 (Phone & FAX)
PO Box 2076
Boulder CO 80306-2076
wilmartr@colorado.edu

Annual Chapbook contest: winners receive 10 percent of press run (determined by number of entries); deadline 10/31; entries must be typeset and bound with clip only; 24 pp. of poetry or prose, bio, acknowledgments and SASE (no restrictions on style or content); simultaneous submissions accepted; reading fee $8 (make checks payable to *Dead Metaphor Press*); winning ms. will be assigned an ISBN number and listed in Books In Print; distributed by Small Press Distribution. Sample chapbooks are available for $6 postpaid.

Naomi Horii, Editor
Many Mountains Moving
303.939.8440 ext.135
303.444.6510 (FAX)
420 22nd Street
Boulder CO 80302
Mmminc@cris.com
Web Site: www.concentric.net/~mmminc

A literary journal of diverse contemporary voices welcomes submissions for its annual literary awards. Send SASE to Naomi Horii, *Many Mountains Moving* Awards, at address above for contest guidelines. Prize $200.

MoonRabbit Review
2525 Arapahoe Avenue • Suite E4-230
Boulder CO 80302
303.4397285
303.439.8362 (FAX)
E-mail: moonrabbit @earthlink.net
Web Site: http://spot.colorado.edu/~jangd/moonrabbit

A bi-annual literary journal of Asian Pacific American voices, featuring poetry, fiction, essays, reviews and artwork in a variety of media from writers residing in the U.S. and Canada. Writer Marilyn Chin will judge the upcoming poetry/fiction contest with over $700 in prize money. Deadline for the contest and for regular submissions is January 15. Previously unpublished works only: submit hard copy, b&w photo, cover letter & brief bio.

One-year subscription rates are: $13/individual; $20/institutions. ***MoonRabbit Review*** is available at all Barnes & Noble book stores, Tattered Cover, and the Boulder Bookstore. For more information, send SASE or E-mail.

Sandy Whelchel, Executive Director
National Writer's Association
303.751.7844
303.751.8593 (FAX)
1450 S. Havana St., Suite 424
Aurora CO 80012

The National Writers' Association is a service organization for writers at all levels and in all disciplines. Many of our 3,000 members are poets as well as writers in other areas. NWA memberships are $65 for Regular, $85 for Professional, and $35 for students with ID.

NWA Poetry Contest runs from July 1 to October 1 yearly. Poetry in all areas is accepted. 40 line limit. Entry fee $8. Judges rating sheets are returned to the author for an SASE. Critiques are optional. 1st-4th places are cash prizes and a copy of the yearly anthology which includes the top three entries in the poetry, short story and nonfiction contests. 5th-10th places receive copy of anthology.

COLORADO SPRINGS

Sherrill Britton, Executive Director
PEN Center USA West
213.365.8500
672 S. Lafayette Park Pl., Suite 41
Los Angeles CA 90057

$1,000 awards to writers west of the Mississippi whose works were published in the preceding year. Novels, poetry books, short stories and translations (of a book of poetry, fiction, or creative nonfiction from any language) are eligible. Publishers, agents or authors must submit four copies of each title by Dec. 31.

PEN Colorado: A regional chapter of PEN USA/West (Los Angeles)
719.262.3562
719.262.3146 (FAX)
Robert Dassanowsky: Pres. PEN Colorado
c/o Dept. of Languages and Cultures
University of Colorado
1420 Austin Bluffs
Colorado Springs CO 80933
e-mail: rvondass@mail.uccs.edu
Web Site: http://www.uccs.edu/~rvondass/pen.html

DENVER AREA

Kimberly Taylor, Executive Director
Megan Maguire
303.839.8323
Colorado Center For the Book
303.866.6976
303.866.6940 (FAX)
2123 Downing St.
Denver CO 80205

The Colorado Book Awards (CBA), a project of the Colorado Center for the Book (chartered by the Library of Congress), are given annually to Colorado authors who exemplify the best writing in the state during a given year. The purpose of the CBA is to champion all Colorado authors and in particular to honor the award winners and promote their titles throughout Colorado and the nation. The Book Awards help build a reputation for Colorado as a state whose people promote and support reading, writing and literacy through books. Entry Rules: Authors must have been a Colorado resident for three of the last twelve months prior to publication year end. Entries may be made by the author, publisher, or anyone with an interest in having a given title submitted for consideration. Entry fee is $30. Entry deadline is Dec. 1. Each entry must include six copies of the book or ms. Books will not be returned. Each entry submitted must include an entry form and be sent to address above. Any book on any subject matter will be considered. The awards committee reserves the right to determine new awards categories based on books submitted and to change the category of any entry. Colorado Book Awards judges, board members and staff of the Colorado Center for the Book, and senior executives of marketing and promotion or public relations departments of sponsoring organizations are ineligible for the award.

Daniel Salazar, Associate Director
Colorado Council on the Arts
303.894.2619
303.894.2615 (FAX)
800.291.ARTS (Toll Free)
750 Pennsylvania Street
Denver CO 80203.3699
daniel.salazar@ossinc.net

The Colorado Council on the Arts presents the Artist Fellowship Awards: an annual fellowship award that provides recognition and funding support to outstanding Colorado artists in performing arts, media arts, visual arts and literature (including poetry, fiction/nonfiction and playwriting/screenwriting) on a rotating cycle. Please contact Daniel Salazar, Associate Director of the CCA, for more information.

Mari Christie, Contact
Denver Press Club
Thomas Hornsby Ferril Poetry Prize
1330 Glenarm
Denver CO 80204

The Thomas Hornsby Ferril Poetry Prize is awarded for a collection of poems by a Colorado poet. Presented annually in conjunction with the Press Club's yearly Ferril benefit reading, which helps support various literary organizations in Colo. Three cash prizes: $250, $150, $100 and a one-year membership to Press Club. First place winner invited to read at the Ferril benefit reading. Must be a resident of Colo. A max. of five unpublished poems (no more than 10 pp.). Two copies, one with author's name, address & phone in upper right hand corner, one without. Handwritten submissions will not be considered. Only one collection per poet. Each submission must be accompanied by a $10 entry fee payable to the Denver Press Club, an entry form, SASE for return of ms. (postage must cover return). Submissions postmarked no later than Sept. 15; winner notified Feb. 1.

Jane Lewis, Public Affairs
Kaiser Permanente
303.344.7244
10350 East Dakota Ave.
Denver CO 80231-1314

Annual Holiday Card Poetry Contest. Poem must be original, eight lines or less & express a holiday message appropriate for vendors and friends of Kaiser. One entry per poet. Prize is $150, recognition, and 100 free cards. Deadline: mid-Sept.

EVERGREEN

Buffalo Bones
Evergreen Poets & Writers
PO Box 714
Evergreen CO 80437

Buffalo Bones is a nonprofit Colorado publication of poetry and prose, begun to provide a forum in which local writers could be published. National Contest prizes: $100 first; $50 second. We publish known and unknown poets. Because we have a rotating editorship, your poem will be read many times.

FORT COLLINS

David Milofsky, Editor
Colorado Review
970.223.4133
970.491.5601 (FAX)
CSU Dept. of English • 359 Eddy Bldg.
Ft. Collins CO 80526
creview@vines.colostate.edu

Annual "Colorado Prize for Poetry" contest (write for guidelines).

Lisa D. Knudsen, Executive Director
Mountains & Plains Booksellers Ass'n.
Regional Book Awards
970.484.5856
805 LaPorte Ave.
Ft. Collins CO 80521

$500 annual award for a book set in the Mountains and Plains region (Ariz., Colo., Idaho, Kan., Tex., Utah, Wyo.): fiction, poetry & nonfiction. Publishers and booksellers may nominate books throughout the year; deadline is Nov. 1.

TELLURIDE

Art Goodtimes, Contact
Telluride Writers Guild
970.327.4767
970.327.4775
PO Box 1008
Telluride CO 81435
goodtimes@infozone.org

Poetry Prize awarded annually to Telluride School students in honor of deceased English teacher and poet, Duane Clark. The Mark Fischer Poetry Prize is awarded annually to a poet in San Miguel County in honor of deceased attorney and poet Mark Fischer.

See listing under **Readings** for the Toads in the Garden poetry series at The Daily Grind: Auraria Campus.

BOULDER

Naropa Institute
Writing & Poetics
303.546.3568
303.546.5297 (FAX)
303.444.0202 (Main)
2130 Arapahoe Ave.
Boulder CO 80302
medgar@naropa.edu
Web Site: www.naropa.edu

The Naropa Institute offers the Jack Kerouac School of Disembodied Poetics. Accredited by North Central Association of Colleges and Schools. Degrees offered: MFA in Writing & Poetics with concentrations in Poetry & Prose; Bachelor's Degree in Writing and Literature; Summer Writing Program. Call for on-going schedule of readings and events.

DENVER AREA

Christopher T. Ransick
Arapahoe Community College
303.797.5857
2500 W. College Dr.
Littleton CO 80160-9002
CRansick@Arapahoe.edu

Accredited college courses in Creative Writing every semester at Arapahoe Community College. See also Publications: ***Progenitor.***

Jana Clark, Head of Creative Writing Dept.
Denver School of the Arts
303.722.4669
303.764.6917 (FAX)
150 S. Pearl St.
Denver CO 80209

6th-12th grade students; audition required for young poets & writers. Publishes two annual magazines comprised of student poetry.

LOVELAND

Evan Oakley
Aims Community College
970.667.4611 ext.332
Loveland CO

Poets in the Park at Foote Lagoon is an annual celebration of poetry held every summer in Loveland, supported by Aims Community College.

PUEBLO

Betsy Morgan
Pueblo Community College
English Department
719.549.3462
719.549.3309 (FAX)
900 W. Orman Ave.
Pueblo CO 81004
morgan@pcc.cccoes.edu

Creative writing and poetry writing courses offered throughout the year; sponsors an annual Festival of Language, presentations of original student work.

Dr. Will Hochman
University of Southern Colorado
English Department
719.549.2077
719.549.2705 (FAX)
2200 Bonforte Blvd.
Pueblo CO 81001
hochman@uscolo.edu
www.uscolo.edu/hungryeye

Sponsors annual local women's poetry prize competition. Hosts poetry readings and workshops. Sponsors student poetry publication: ***The Hungry Eye.*** Offers creative writing classes. Postings.

COLORADO SPRINGS

Katherine Douglass, Director
First Night Pikes Peak
719.329.7265
Downtown Colorado Springs CO

Annual event for families from 5 p.m.-midnight: poets and all types of artists, including dancers, musicians and dramatists, are encouraged to apply. Deadline for applications is August 30.

Mary Mashburn, Contact
The Imagination Celebration
Pikes Peak Library District
719.531.6333 ext. 1208
719.528.2820 (FAX)
5550 N. Union
Colorado Springs CO 80918
mmashbur@ppld.org

The Imagination Celebration sponsors a poetry contest for children and a variety of poetry (and other arts-related events) for children in schools and other venues. Ongoing throughout the school year, but with a major focus in April.

DENVER

Kimberly Taylor, Executive Director
Megan Maguire, Contact
303.839.8323
Colorado Center For the Book
303.866.6976
303.866.6940 (FAX)
2123 Downing St.
Denver CO 80205

The Colorado Center for the Book (CCFTB) envisions a state where all people are literate, and there is a community focus on the joy of reading and support of books and the book arts. Our vision is to encourage all people to learn and develop the life skills necessary to be responsible, creative citizens and to enhance their quality of life. CCFTB takes an active role in promoting reading and writing as a value in Colorado. We produce highly visible promotional activities and form partnerships with organizations sharing similar goals. We seek to increase understanding of the vital roles educators, librarians, writers, publishers, booksellers, and book artists play in attaining our vision of literacy and the celebration of books and the written word. The Center for the Book holds a variety of other events throughout the year for Colorado authors and poets. The Rocky Mountain Book Festival is an annual event that features published poets in workshops, panel discussions and readings. If you are interested in participating, please call Megan Maguire.

SETH
RANDOM AXE OF RHYME
303.458.7952
3238 CLAY ST.
DENVER CO 80211

Hosted by the Open Rangers and Jafrika, "Random Axe of Rhyme" is a monthly showcase for performance poets and other creative artists. Shows begin at 8 p.m. the first Sat. of every month at the Bug Performance and Media Art Center, 3654 Navajo St., Denver, CO 80211. For ticket info call 303.477.5977 or 303.458.7952.

LOVELAND

EVAN OAKLEY
POETS IN THE PARK
AIMS COMMUNITY COLLEGE
970.667.4611 EXT.332
LOVELAND CO

Poets in the Park at Foote Lagoon is an annual celebration of poetry held every summer in Loveland, supported by Aims Community College. This full-day event brings together nationally known poets, regional poets, literature lovers, academics, students and the public in a variety of formats: featured readings, seminars, workshops, student readings, children's classes and children's readings. Poets in the Park has featured such outstanding national and local poets as Joy Harjo, Carolyn Forché, Rita Keifer, Tony Park, Li-Young Lee and Colorado Poet Laureate, Mary Crow. The festival, which is free and open to the public, is a testament to the enduring appeal of poetry.

BOULDER

Marty Durlin, Station Manager
KGNU
303.449.4885
800.737.3030 (Toll Free)
1900 Folsom, Suite 100
PO Box 885
Boulder CO 80306-0885

Community radio station owned by Boulder Community Broadcast Ass'n. 88.5MHz. Spoken Word program, "Art Allowed" airs on Mon. from 8-9 p.m.

COLORADO SPRINGS

Jim Ciletti, Contact
La Dolce Vita
719.632.1369
333 N. Tejon
Colorado Springs CO 80903

Performances & Workshops vary, as do dates and times. Call for more information.

DENVER

The Bug
303.477.5977
3654 Navajo St.
Denver CO 80211

The Bug presents "Random Axe of Rhyme" poetry and multi-media presentation on the first Sat. of each month at 7:30 p.m., featuring Jafrika & the Open Rangers.

SETH
303.458.7952
Denver Press Club
1330 Glenarm
Denver CO 80204

Monthly poetry performance every 2nd Sat. Just starting in 1997, call for more details.

Marge Tanaiwaki, Contact
Making Waves: Asians in Action
303.333.2130
303.592.1510 (FAX)
6100 E. Severn Pl.
Denver CO 80220

Readers theater that occasionally incorporates poetry.

BOULDER

Bess Holloway, Publisher/Editor
Hazel Hart, Editor
ARRAY
303.440.4207
3575 28th St. #104
Boulder CO 80301-1539

Published annually each Nov. beg. in 1997 (formerly three times a year). 15 issues published between 1992 and 1997. Reading Period: July 1-Sept. 15. Material Printed: poetry (18-30 lines), short fiction, personal essays; Size: 8.5 x 5.5 inches, 28-32 pages; Payment in copies (1 per poem; 2 for material occupying more than 2 pgs.); 100-120 free copies distributed to contributors and bookstores in Boulder & Wichita.

John Kellow, Literary Arts Editor
Boulder Planet
303.444.5761
303.415.1210 (FAX)
2028 14th St.
Boulder CO 80302

A free weekly periodical with a literary arts section. Poetry is published twice monthly. The BP accepts submissions from Colorado writers **only** of poetry up to 150 lines (max. of six poems). Must submit hard copy and 3.5" floppy in text format (include SASE for return). Allow six months response time.

Naomi Horii, Editor
Many Mountains Moving
303.939.8440 ext.135
303.444.6510 (FAX)
420 22nd Street
Boulder CO 80302
Mmminc@cris.com
Web Site: www.concentric.net/~mmminc

Many Mountains Moving: a literary journal of diverse contemporary voices welcomes poetry from Colorado poets from all backgrounds. Please address submissions c/o Alissa Norton. Include SASE for reply/return. Sample copy $6.50.

MoonRabbit Review
2525 Arapahoe Avenue
Suite E4-230
Boulder CO 80302
303.4397285
303.439.8362 (FAX)
E-mail: moonrabbit @earthlink.net
Web Site: http://spot.colorado.edu/~jangd/moonrabbit

A bi-annual literary journal of Asian Pacific American voices, featuring poetry, fiction, essays, reviews and artwork in a variety of media from writers residing in the U.S. and Canada. One-year subscription rates are: $13/individual; $20/institutions. ***MoonRabbit Review*** is available at all Barnes & Nobles, Tattered Cover & the Boulder Bookstore. For more information, send SASE or E-mail.

Jim Cohn, Editor
Napalm Health Spa
Bios Angelikos Press
303.444.4490
3000 Colorado Blvd. E-219
Boulder CO 80303
jimcohn@ecentral.com

Annual poetry publication made of handmade paper. Submission requirements: max. of 10 poems with SASE; Deadline Dec. 31; Published in April: $30/issue

COLORADO SPRINGS

Elizabeth Smith: 719.636.1257
Lois Hayna: 719.599.0502
John Thelin: 719.578.5909
the eleventh MUSE
Poetry West
PO Box 2143
Colorado Springs CO 80901

Poetry West is a nonprofit organization that welcomes new members. Dues are $25/year. ***the eleventh MUSE*** accepts submissions of three to five poems, any style. Send submissions c/o Poetry West in a #10 envelope (no oversized manila envelopes); SASE required. Copies of ***the eleventh MUSE*** are available at Colorado Spgs. bookstores or $4.50 ppd. by mail order.

Dr. Alex Blackburn
Writers' Forum
University of Colorado
719.599.4023
719.593.3362 (FAX)
PO Box 7150
Colorado Springs CO 80933-7150

DENVER AREA

Peggy R. Leppek, Editor
Denver Word Affiliate
303.831.7452
PO Box 2913
Denver CO 80201-2913

Denver Word Affiliate is designed to create new opportunities and projects for writers, to unite a community of wordists, to recruit an inclusive membership, to form a collective effort, to be respectful of all work, to encourage participants to promote poetic expression/diversity. DWA publishes a bi-monthly poetry newsletter called ***Denver Word***. Membership: $15 (newsletter only); $35 Individual; $100 Group/Patron.

Dr. Robert O. Greer, Publisher
High Plains Literary Review
303.320.6828
180 Adams St., Suite 250
Denver CO 80206

A nonprofit publication, published three times a year (April, Aug., Dec.). Only previously unpublished work will be considered. Manuscripts are read year-round and submission is open to all writers. Unsolicited manuscripts must be accompanied by SASE. Address all inquiries to The Editors. Subscriptions: $20 a year; $38 for 2 years. Single copies are $7.

Cale Kenney, Editor
Howlings: Wild Women of the West
Tell Tale Publishing
303.355.6601
PO Box 6004
Denver CO 80206

A regional literary magazine for writers in Denver and the Rocky Mountain region. Sponsors contests and supports local women poets, fiction and non-fiction writers. 66 pp.; over 100 writers published. Frequency: 4 x year. For more information on contest and submission guidelines, submit SASE to address above or send $7 for a sample copy (***Howlings*** is available for $6.50 at select Denver bookstores.)

Peggy DeForest-Stalls, Editor
Inner 303
2100 Stout St.
Denver CO 80205
303.291.0442
303.295.3599 (FAX)

A zine dedicated to publishing the creative works of inner-city youth ages 14-24. Accepts submissions from youth across the nation (submissions cannot be returned); produced at The Spot, a nonprofit urban youth creative center in Denver.

Michael J. Henry & Andrea Dupree
The Lighthouse Inkwell
Lighthouse Writers, Inc.
303.297.1185 (Phone & FAX)
2000 Arapahoe St., Suite 205
Denver CO 80205
AEDupree@aol.com

Lighthouse Writers originated in Boston, MA, and is now dedicated to broadening access to serious writing classes/workshops to all poets/writers in Colo. Newsletter: ***The Lighthouse Inkwell*** (announces publications and/or events). Circ.: 100.

Padma Thornlyre
Mad Blood
303.215.1624
303.239.8428 (FAX)
17752 W. 14th Ave. #9
Golden CO 80401
padmat@rmc.org

Publishes broadsheet of poetry called ***Mad Blood***.

Scott Sawyer, Editor
Joy Sawyer, Poetry Editor
Mars Hill Review
303.643.1885
303.832.9293 (FAX)
800.990.MARS (Toll Free)
11757 W. Ken Caryl Ave., Suite F330
Littleton CO 80127-3700
mars.hill@pobox.com

Mars Hill Review attempts to articulate a refreshing theology of hope by publishing essays, fiction, poetry & reviews that reflect a thoughtful Christian worldview. Recent poets published in ***MHR*** include: Scott Cairns, Walt McDonald, Luci Shaw, Jean Janzen, Paul Willis, Brian Dietrich, John Leax.

Christopher T. Ransick
Progenitor
Arapahoe Community College
303.797.5857
2500 W. College Dr.
Littleton CO 80160-9002
CRansick@Arapahoe.edu

Progenitor: annual, award-winning art and literary magazine of Arapahoe Community College.

Eric Hjerstedt Sharp, Contact
Sharptongue
Sharp Tongue Press
303.446.2222
303.572.3940 (FAX)
819 Delaware, Suite 1
Denver CO 80204
stpltd@netway.net
Web Site: www.geocities.com/SoHo/Studios/1307

Sharptongue is a twice-monthly publication that aims to provide the Denver poetry community with a reading calendar, chapbook reviews, and news regarding Denver poets and events. ***Sharptongue*** welcomes short news items and poems.

Tom Auer, Publisher/Editor-in-Chief
The Bloomsbury Review
303.863.0406
303.863.0408 (FAX)
1762 Emerson St.
Denver CO 80218-1012

Ivan Suvanjieff, Publisher
Lee Christopher, Executive Editor
303.215.0791
The New Censorship Magazine
Web Site: www.PeaceJam.org

GLENWOOD SPRINGS

Jon Rietfors, Publisher/Editor
AKA Publications
970.928.8344
311 Laurel #1
Glenwood Springs CO 81601
jrietfor@rof.net

A sporadic publication: publishes poetry that meets theme requirements.

EVERGREEN

Buffalo Bones
Evergreen Poets & Writers
PO Box 714
Evergreen CO 80437

A nonprofit Colorado publication of poetry & prose, begun to provide a forum in which local writers could be published. ***Buffalo Bones*** publishes a National Issue 1x/yr. and a Western & Regional Issue 2x/yr. Subscriptions available for $12/yr. (4 issues); sponsorships of an issue ("Friends of Evergreen Poets and Writers") available for $25—name of group or organization will be acknowledged in that issue. ***Buffalo Bones*** is 50 pp. digest size. Submit up to five poems, any form; 40 line limit. Deadline for National Issue: Jan. 15; deadlines for Regional Issue: July 1 & Oct. 15. Looking for narratives with a twist, strong imagery, short poems with a punch, a bit of fun now and then. ***Buffalo Bones*** does not print poems that are vulgar, sexually explicit, profane or woe-is-me.

FORT COLLINS

David Milofsky, Editor
Colorado Review
CSU Dept. of English
970.223.4133
970.491.5601 (FAX)
359 Eddy Bldg.
Ft. Collins CO 80526
creview@vines.colostate.edu

Magazine published bi-annually. Publishes poetry and sponsors an annual "Colorado Prize for Poetry" (write for guidelines).

PUEBLO

John Demus
Pueblo Arts Council
719.543.8112
PO Box 4005
Pueblo CO 81003

The ***Arts About Pueblo*** monthly newsletter promotes collaborations among artists, poets and musicians.

TELLURIDE

Telluride Daily Planet
970.728.9788
Box 2315
Telluride CO 81435
Web Site: www.telluridegateway.com

Publishes weekly poem in "Up Bear Creek," a column by Art Goodtimes.

BOULDER

Marty Durlin, Station Manager
KGNU Radio
303.449.4885
800.737.3030 (Toll Free)
1900 Folsom, Suite 100
PO Box 885
Boulder CO 80306-0885

Community radio station owned by Boulder Community Broadcast Association. 88.5MHz. Spoken Word program, "Art Allowed" airs on Mon. from 8-9 p.m.

PUEBLO

John Demus
KRRU Radio (1480 AM)
719.542.4277
4211 N. Elizabeth
Pueblo CO 81003

Radio show from 5-6 p.m. every Thursday, featuring local and area poets and musicians.

BOULDER

Jim, Manager
Aion Bookshop
303.443.5763
1235 Pennsylvania Ave.
Boulder CO 80302
Aionbook@interloc.com

Hosts Naropa Institute student readings. Call for more information.

Naomi Horii, Editor
Many Mountains Moving
303.939.8440
420 22nd Street
Boulder CO 80302
Mmminc@cris.com

Many Mountains Moving: a literary journal of diverse contemporary voices is launching a reading series. Call 303.545.9942 for further information.

Mary Jo, Manager
Penny Lane Coffeehouse
303.443.9516
1795 Pearl St.
Boulder CO 80302

Poetry reading every Mon.: Sept.1 through May 30: from 8-11 p.m.; June/July/Aug.: from 9 p.m.-midnight. Hosted by Tom Peters.

Dr. James Hutchinson
Rocky Mountain Writer's Guild
Live Poets' Society
303.444.4100
837 15th St.
Boulder CO 80302

Organization meets monthly; must be selected to be in the society. Poetry society readings and criticism held the second Fri. of every month, 7-10 p.m.

COLORADO SPRINGS

Chris Tauscher, Contact
Barnes & Noble Bookstore
719.637.8282
795 Citadel Dr. East
Colorado Springs CO 80909

Open readings & occasional guest readers on the first Fri. of each month from 7-8:30 p.m.

Elizabeth Smith: 719.636.1257
Lois Hayna: 719.599.0502
John Thelin: 719.578.5909
Poetry West
P.O. Box 2143
Colorado Springs CO 80901

Poetry West is a nonprofit organization dedicated to bringing poetry workshops and readings to the Pikes Peak region. All workshops and readings are free and open to the public and usually are held on the first Fri. and/or Sat. of each month. Locations and local/visiting poet speakers vary. Poetry West welcomes new members. Dues are $25/year. Poetry West also provides occasional workshops and/or readings for various groups, including senior citizens, schools, prisons and detention centers.

Richard Skorman, Owner
Poor Richard's Restaurant/Bookstore
719.578.0012 (5549)
719.632.7721
320 N. Tejon
Colorado Springs CO 80903

Open readings & "Bare Knuckle Poetry" every third Tues. of the month from 7-10 p.m.

Amy Daniel, Contact
Wooglin's Deli
719.578.9443
823 N. Teton
Colorado Springs CO 80903

Open readings every Tues. from 7 to 10:30 p.m.

DENVER AREA

Henry Alarmclock, Host
Across the Street Café
303.813.9908
3242 E. Colfax Ave.
Denver CO

Open poetry reading Tues. nights from 7-10 p.m. Sign-up sheet format.

SETH, Host
303.458.7952
Denver Press Club
1330 Glenarm
Denver CO 80204

Monthly poetry performance every 2nd Sat. Just starting in 1997, call for details.

Frank Winters, Host
Flesh Poetics. Marija Cerjak Society
303.286.1818
Commerce City CO 80022-2502

The Marija Cerjak Society open reading is held every Tues. at the Denver Book Mall, 32 Broadway, Denver, at 8 p.m. Hosted by Frank Winters. $5

Padma Thornlyre, Contact
Mad Blood Soirée
303.215.1624
303.239.8428 (FAX)

Presents occasional readings called the Mad Blood Soirée (locations and times vary).

Marilynn Magenity, Owner
Mercury Cafe
303.294.9281
303.294.9258
2199 California St.
Denver CO 80205

Readings held every Wed. at 8 p.m. and at 10 p.m. on Fri., hosted by Ed Ward.

Ann Miller, Host: 303.279.7373
Jane Browning: 303.279.7095
Poetry & More
915 19th St.
Golden CO 80401
amiller@spot.colorado.edu

Poetry & More sponsors readings of narrative and poetry every other Saturday from 7:30 to 9:30 at Renate's German Bakery, 1301 Arapahoe, Golden. A featured reader is followed by an "open mike". Poetry & More's scheduled readers include Joanne Greenberg, Joe Hutchison, Patricia Dubrava, Marilyn Krysl and Peter Michelson. Poetry & More's mission is to give writers a forum to try out their work and to provide an atmosphere conducive to mentorship between accomplished writers and those who are just beginning. No admission charge.

Eric Hjerstedt Sharp, Host
Poets @ Denver Book Mall
Denver Book Mall
303.446.2222
Denver CO
stpltd@netway.net

Every Sat. at 8 p.m. Hosted by Eric Sharp. $2

Hector Muñoz, Host
Rebis Galleries
303.698.1841
1930 S. Broadway
Denver CO

Reading hosted by Hector Muñoz on the last Sun. of each month. Featured readers at 8 p.m.; open reading at 9 p.m.

Jackie St. Joan, Host
Second Monday Poetry Series
Tattered Cover LoDo
303.436.1070
800.833.9327
1536 Wynkoop St.
Denver CO 80202
newslttr@tatteredcover.com

Our Poetry Series and our exceptional poetry selection invite you to indulge yourself in the pure intensity of poetry. Each month we offer readings by local, regional, and national or international poets. The Second Monday Poetry Series is held on the second Monday of the month and takes place in the LoDo store at 7:30 p.m. Please join us. To receive our Poetry Series flyer, call 322.1965 ext. 2700 or E-mail at address above.

Chris Murphy, Host
Smokin' Spoken Word Jam
Ironworks Brewery & Pub
303.987.3372
12354 Alameda Pkwy.
Lakewood CO

Reading every Tues. Sign up at 7:30 p.m.

Bruce Kauffman, Host
303.722.9944
Toads in the Garden
The Daily Grind Coffeehouse
303.573.JAVA
900 Auraria Pkwy. #240
Tivoli Student Union
Denver CO 80204

A Thursday night poetry series held weekly from September through May, with the exception of campus closures between fall and winter sessions and spring break. The Daily Grind is located on the Auraria Campus in the Tivoli Brewery. All featured readings preceded by open reading; one reading each month devoted exclusively to an open reading. Readings held monthly in June/July/Aug.; $2/$1 with student I.D. (All proceeds help support featured poet.)

DOLORES

Tim & Laurie Wood, Directors
Dolores Bookstore & Coffeehouse
970.882.7105
Box 326
Dolores CO 81323

Host monthly readings for Weed Seed Literary Co-op.

EVERGREEN

Carolyn Wangaard, Contact
303.674.5023
Evergreen Poets & Writers
PO Box 714
Evergreen CO 80437

Evergreen Poets & Writers sponsors poetry readings at the Evergreen Lake House at 7 p.m. 4 x per year: March, May, Oct., Dec. Call for specific dates.

FORT COLLINS

Elaine, Contact
Bas Bleu Theatre Company
970.498.8949
216 Pine St.
Ft. Collins CO 80524

The theatre hosts 10 readings per year. Call contact for more information.

GRAND JUNCTION

Renee & Brent Nelson, Directors
Common Grounds Coffeehouse
970.241.4221
Grand Junction CO

Host occasional poetry readings.

Woody Hildebrant, Host
The Station Art Emporium
970.255.8519
701 Main St.
Grand Junction CO 81501

Open stage for poetry every Tues. at 8 p.m. Any poets interested in featuring at the readings must call Woody at least two to three weeks ahead.

LOVELAND

Tom Katsimpalis, Curator of Interpretation
Loveland Museum and Gallery
970.962.2410
5th & Lincoln
Loveland CO 80537

Presents a poetry series with featured readers in the fall and spring. Contact Tom Katsimpalis for more information.

PUEBLO

Cynthia Ramu, Contact
719.546.0315
Gold Dust Saloon
719.545.0741
130 S. Union Ave.
Pueblo CO 81003

Restaurant sponsors free open poetry readings on the fourth Wednesday of each month at 7 p.m.

Nathan Anderson
New Frontier Coffee House
719.583.0664
624 N. Main
Pueblo CO 81003

Sponsors poetry reading every other Mon. night. Hours of business: Mon.-Sat.; from 8 a.m. to midnight.

TELLURIDE/NORWOOD

Frances Baer, Director
Bear Paw Books & Gifts
970.327.4266
1611 Grand Ave.
Norwood CO 81423

Hosts occasional poetry readings.

Edi Katz, Owner
Between the Covers Bookstore
970.728.4504
224 W. Colorado Ave.
P.O. Box 1439
Telluride CO 81435

Hosts occasional poetry readings and booksignings.

Gina, Director
Bookworks
970.728.0770
191 S. Pine St.
Telluride CO 81435

Hosts occasional poetry readings and booksignings.

Art Goodtimes, Contact
Gourds Circle Reading Series
Telluride Writers Guild
Box 1008
Telluride CO 81435
970.327.4775
goodtimes@infozone.org

Gourds Circle Reading Series presents monthly performances every third Friday of the month with a featured reader/gourd circle afterwards at Wilkinson Library.

Proposed new project: a Bobbie Burns Night, poetry and single malt whiskey tasting (tba in 1998).

WINDSOR

Renée Johnson & Jackie Wiggins, Owners
Books/N/Things
970.686.0583
414A Main St.
Windsor CO 80550

Host featured readings and booksignings on the second and fourth Sat. of every month.

NORTHERN COLORADO/WYOMING

Steven Smith, Contact
Serendipity Poets
307.635.4725
PO Box 6270
Cheyenne, WY 82003
ChySerendp@aol.com

Serendipity Poets provides readings, community projects, contacts, events and performances.

BOULDER

Lisa Gesner, Manager
Boulder Book Store
303.447.2074
303.447.9539 (FAX)
1107 Pearl St.
Boulder CO 80302
BoulderBk@aol.com
Web Site: www.boulderbookstore.com

Boulder Book Store has an ongoing commitment to support local poets & small presses. Sponsors an annual April Poetry Month celebration (poetry readings, giveaways, contest), and an Annual Small Press Reading in early summer. Presents over 100 author events per year and creative writing workshops on an ongoing basis.

Rob Otwell
Brillig Works Café and Bakery
303.444.0814
1322 College Ave.
Boulder CO 80302

Coffeehouse offers boards for postings; possible venue for readings.

Louise Knapp
Word is Out Women's Bookstore
303.449.1415
1713 15th St.
Boulder CO 80302

Sporadic readings. Call for more information.

DENVER AREA

The Daily Grind Coffeehouse
303.573.JAVA
900 Auraria Pkwy. #240
Tivoli Student Union
Denver CO 80204

The Daily Grind is located on the Auraria Campus in the Tivoli Brewery. Toads in the Garden readings each Thurs. (see listing under **Readings**). $2/$1 with student I.D. Venue available for additional artistic endeavors.

Teresa Kishiyama, Owner
Java.net Cybercafe
303.617.7490
303.617.7579 (FAX)
4034 South Parker Rd.
Aurora CO 80014
teresa@java.netcafe.com
Web Site: www.java-netcafe.com

A gourmet coffee shop with computers (17" monitors, Office 95 and full internet connections). java.net cybercafe is a place where poetry artists can meet and exchange ideas or work. If someone would like to hold a reading, we are happy to listen to their ideas and cater to their needs. Another idea is to have poetry framed and displayed in the coffee shop. Contact Teresa for more information or to exchange ideas.

Marilynn Magenity, Owner
Mercury Cafe
303.294.9281
303.294.9258
2199 California St.
Denver CO 80205

See listing under Readings.

Michael Thornton
The Bug
303.477.5977
3654 Navajo St.
Denver CO 80211

Nonprofit, volunteer operated and member supported performance and media art center. The Bug presents Random Axe of Rhyme poetry and multi-media presentation (see listing under Performances) on the first Sat. of each month at 7:30 p.m., featuring Jafrika and the Open Rangers.

FORT COLLINS

Rob Osborne
Avogadro's Number
970.493.5555
970.482.1756
615 S. Mason St.
Ft. Collins CO 80521

Restaurant/Stage Room/Bar/Coffeehouse hosts poetry contests and slams. Owner is interested in hosting poetry readings on a regular basis, if someone offers to facilitate.

Elaine, Contact
Bas Bleu Theatre Company
970.498.8949
216 Pine St.
Ft. Collins CO 80524

The theatre hosts 10 readings per year. Call contact for more information.

Tom Rowland, Owner
Happenstance
970.493.1668
136 W. Mountain Ave.
Ft. Collins CO 80524

Bookstore offers a 10 percent discount to published poets and an extensive poetry selection. Intends to sponsor readings at the store as space allows.

Mark LaFrambois
Stone Lion Bookstore
970.493.0030
107 N. College Ave.
Ft. Collins CO 80524
stonelionbook.com

Hosts authors on tour (readings and booksignings) and occasional readings. Hosts the annual fall reading "Writer's Harvest." Proceeds go to the Larimer County food bank.

GRAND JUNCTION

Renee & Brent Nelson, Directors
Common Grounds Coffeehouse
970.241.4221
Grand Junction CO

Hosts occasional poetry readings.

Woody Hildebrant, Host
The Station Art Emporium
970.255.8519
701 Main St.
Grand Junction CO 81501

Open stage for poetry every Tues. at 8 p.m. Any poets interested in featuring at the readings must call Woody at least two to three weeks ahead.

PUEBLO

Cynthia Ramu, Contact
719.546.0315
Gold Dust Saloon
719.545.0741
130 S. Union Ave.
Pueblo CO 81003

Restaurant sponsors free open poetry readings on the fourth Wednesday of each month at 7 p.m. and original acoustic music on the second Wed. of the month.

Jeanne Gardner, Director
Pueblo Community College
Learning Resources Center
719.549.3308
719.549.3309 (FAX)
900 W. Orman Ave.
Pueblo CO 81004

Sponsors book signings for local authors.

Joanne Dodds
Pueblo Library District
719.543.9600
719.543.9610 (FAX)
100 E. Abnendo
Pueblo CO 81002

Sponsors special events; sponsors a reading of original poetry by local residents for Women's History Week; postings; meeting rooms available for poetry activities.

TELLURIDE

Robin Machado, Director
Wilkinson Library
970.728.6613
134 S. Spruce St.
Telluride CO 81435

Projects: Gourd Circle Reading Series: hosts site for TWG's monthly readings

Writers in the Sky: local literary sojourn including poet Simon Ortiz. Oct. 25, 1997. Director: Ann Kennedy

Poets in Person: four week program featuring work of Allen Ginsburg, Sharon Olds, Gary Soto, and Rita Dove in October; from 7-9 p.m. Director: Rosemerry Wahtola Trommer. Call for specific dates.

BOULDER

Laurie Kay Olson
Poetry Society of Colorado, Inc.
303.449.1325
2635 Mapleton #10
Boulder CO 80304

Workshops on the first Tues. of every month at 1 p.m., Sept. through May, at the Ilios Restaurant, 1201 Broadway, Denver. Topics range from forms to marketing.

COLORADO SPRINGS

Jim Ciletti, Contact
La Dolce Vita
719.632.1369
333 N. Tejon
Colorado Springs CO 80903

Bookstore/Coffeehouse: Performances and workshops vary, as do groups, events, styles, dates and times. Call for more information.

Elizabeth Smith: 719.636.1257
Lois Hayna: 719.599.0502
John Thelin: 719.578.5909
Poetry West
PO Box 2143
Colorado Springs CO 80901

Poetry West is a nonprofit organization dedicated to bringing poetry workshops and readings to the Pikes Peak region. All are free and open to the public and usually are held on the first Fri. and/or Sat. of the month. Locations and poet speakers vary. Poetry West welcomes new members. Dues are $25/year. Poetry West also provides occasional workshops and/or readings for various groups, including senior citizens, schools, prisons and detention centers.

DENVER AREA

Anita Jepson-Gilbert: 303.465.0883
Margaret Walther: 303.755.3638
Columbine Poetry Society
Poets of the Foothills Art Center
10751 Routt St.
Broomfield CO 80021
wagil@aol.com

Columbine Poets is the official state poetry society for Colorado, affiliated with the National Federation of State Poetry Societies. Membership is open to any resident of Colorado interested in poetry. State membership dues of $8 entitle membership in the National Federation, as well. There currently are two chapters in Colorado: the Foothills chapter and the Evergreen chapter. Poetry writing classes offered each Sat., 10am-12 noon (call for details). Critiquing workshops are held every 3rd Sun. of the month at 1:30 p.m. (call Margaret Walther).

Michael J. Henry & Andrea Dupree
Lighthouse Writers, Inc.
303.297.1185 (Phone & FAX)
2000 Arapahoe St., Suite 205
Denver CO 80205
AEDupree@aol.com

Lighthouse Writers originated in Boston, and is dedicated to broadening access to serious writing classes and workshops to all poets/writers in Colorado. We have taught for several years at Emerson College & Northeastern University. Weekly, two-hour creative writing workshops, on-going. Call for complete list of offerings. Exclusively poetry and all-women workshops offered periodically; cross-genre workshops on-going. Meet at our Bayly loft space: 20th and Arapahoe (occasional meetings at local cafes where we host open mikes). Facilitated by poet Michael J. Henry and fiction writer Andrea Dupree. Free community writing workshops held bi-monthly at Denver Public Library.

Eric Hjerstedt Sharp, Contact
Sharp Tongue Press
303.446.2222
303.572.3940 (FAX)
819 Delaware, Suite 1
Denver CO 80204
stpltd@netway.net
Web Site: www.geocities.com/SoHo/Studios/1307

Sharptongue Writers Workshop at the Denver Book Mall on Tues. at 6 p.m.

Lois Harvey
West Side Books
303.561.0035
303.480.5193 (FAX)
3600 West 32nd Ave., Suite C
Denver CO 80211
cellebooklh@aol.com

Writers workshop meets on Sundays. Must call, classes fill quickly. Will be hosting readings in the future (just relocated).

Nancy Vorkink
Poet/Teacher
303.863.8449
1535 Franklin St. #6KL
Denver CO 80218
Javarose@plinet.com

Poetry 101 workshops for non-profits. Usually 8-week modules; fee is negotiable.

PUEBLO

Donna Stinchcomb
Sangre De Cristo Arts & Conference Center
719.543.0130
719.543.0134 (FAX)
210 N. Santa Fe
Pueblo CO 81003

Sponsors poetry writing workshops.

TELLURIDE

Judy Kohin, Director
Ah Haa School For the Arts
970.728.3886
135 S. Spruce St.
PO Box 1590
Telluride CO 81435

Hosts various readings and performances; co-sponsors Talking Gourds events.

ASPEN

Jeannie, Director
Julie Comins, Contact
Aspen Writers' Foundation
Red Brick Arts & Recreation Center
970.925.3122
970.970.5700 (FAX)
800.925.2526 (Toll Free)
110 East Hallam St.
Aspen CO 81612
Aspenwrite@aol.com

The Aspen Writers' Group offers a weekly workshop that includes readings and discussion by participants. All writers are welcome.

DENVER AREA

Anita Jepson-Gilbert, Contact
303.465.0883
Margaret Walther
303.755.3638
Columbine Poetry Society
Poets of the Foothills Art Center
10751 Routt St.
Broomfield CO 80021
wagil@aol.com

Columbine Poets is the official state poetry society for Colorado, affiliated with the National Federation of State Poetry Societies. Membership is open to any resident of Colorado interested in poetry. State membership dues of $8 entitles membership in the National Federation, as well. There currently are two chapters in Colorado: the Foothills chapter and the Evergreen chapter. Poetry writing classes offered each Saturday, 10am-12 noon (call for details). Critiquing workshops are held every 3rd Sunday of the month at 1:30 p.m. (call Margaret Walther for details).

Kay Adams, Poetry Therapist
Paula Hagar, Contact
303.329.0943
Whole Body Health
303.421.2298
198 Union Blvd. #210
Lakewood CO 80228
KayAdams@aol.com

Poetry Peer Circle, second Sunday of each month from 1:30-4:30 p.m. All are welcome to create and share poetry in a warm, non-judgmental, non-critical group setting. No experience or background needed. Near 6th & Simms in Lakewood. Call Paula Hagar or Kay Adams for information. Associated with the National

Ass'n. for Poetry Therapy, a multidisciplinary professional organization for helping professionals, educators, poets, writers. Educational, networking and credentialing opportunities in developmental and/or clinical poetry therapy. Alicia Seeger, NAPT, PO Box 551, Port Washington NY 11050; www.poetrytherapy.org.

STEAMBOAT SPRINGS

Harriet Freiberger, Director
Steamboat Springs Writers Group
970.879.8079
970.879.9062
PO Box 774284
Steamboat Springs CO 80477
freiberger@compuserve.com

Steamboat Springs Writers Group, sponsored by Steamboat Springs Arts Council, meets weekly to discuss and critique poetry, fiction and non-fiction. Everyone is welcome.

NUCLA

Ruth Sampson, Director
West End Literary Guild
Workshop Ceramic Studio
970.864.2176
838 Main St.
Nucla CO 81424

Occasional gatherings for writers and poets.

EDITING

Catherine O'Neill Thorn, Owner
O'Neill Publishing
303.697.1317
303.697.9799 (FAX)
PO Box 53
Indian Hills CO 80454
ONeillPub@aol.com
Publishing, Editing & Writing

Professional Quality • Personal Service • Reasonable Rates
Typesetting/Page Layout & Design, including word processing; Editing and Poetry Consultation; Free-lance writing. 10 percent discount to poets who mention this listing.

Tim McMahon, Owner
Ruah Graphics
303.831.7415
1301 Lafayette St. Unit 2
Denver CO 80218

Desktop publishing, editing, page layout and design, printing referral and pre-press. 10 percent discount on any poetry job with the mention of this listing.

Ron Jaeger
303.699.9679
4117.D S. Mobile Cr., Unit D
Aurora CO 80013
Poiesis001@aol.com

National poetry judge and regularly published poetry reviewer is now accepting manuscripts to edit or critique. Just one critique of one poem will put an unpublished poet on the path to publication.

EVENTS PRODUCTION

G and H, Contacts
Grant R. Productions
970/785-0912
P.O. Box 33267
Denver CO 80233
spokenwd@grantrproductions.com

Avant Garde Entertainment Agency: producers of special events. We put on any size show for any size budget. We represent an interesting assortment of underground performance poets, artists, and musicians. Always accepting demo submissions.

GRAPHIC DESIGN

Lynn Brewer, Owner
XL Services
PO Box 3023
Evergreen CO 80437
303.670.9000

Digital imaging; graphic design; photography. 10 percent discount to poets mentioning this listing.

Linda Bevard, Owner
One At A Time Press
303.458.6903
4321 Winona Ct.
Denver CO 80212

Hand-set type and letterpress printing of short poems. 20 percent discount to any poet mentioning this listing.

Robert Howard, Owner
Robert Howard Graphic Design
970.225.0083
631 Manfield Dr.
Ft. Collins CO 80525

Book design for chapbooks and poetry books. 10 percent discount to Colorado poets mentioning this listing.

Tim McMahon, Owner
Ruah Graphics
303.831.7415
1301 Lafayette St. Unit 2
Denver CO 80218

Desktop publishing, editing, page layout and design, printing referral and prepress. 10 percent discount on any poetry job with the mention of this listing.

PRINTERS

Scott Laudenslager, Owner
KIMCO Reprographics
303/295-1172
303.295.2754 (FAX)
4120 Brighton Blvd., Suite A21
Denver CO 80216

Poetry is usually published in collections, and we *specialize* in short-run books. Full-service commercial printer, includes printing of broadsheets and postcards. KIMCO is a long-time supporter of poetry.

Linda Bevard, Owner
One At A Time Press
303.458.6903
4321 Winona Ct.
Denver CO 80212

Hand-set type and letterpress printing of short poems. 20 percent discount to any poet mentioning this listing.

PUBLISHERS

Paul Dilsaver
Blue Light Review
PO Box 1621
Pueblo CO 81002

Not currently accepting submissions. Back issues of the poetry magazine, ***Blue Light Review***, available.

Blue Mountain Arts
Editorial Dept.
303.449.0536
PO Box 1007, Dept. PG
Boulder CO 80306-1007
bma@rmi.net
Web Site: www.bluemountainarts.com

Interested in reviewing poetry appropriate for greeting cards. We suggest you familiarize yourself with our products first. Seek original, sensitive poetry and prose on love, friendship, family, and the challenges and aspirations of life; writings on special occasions (birthday, anniversary, etc.), as well as Christmas, Easter, Mother's Day, Father's Day. All ms. submissions and questions should be directed in writing. Please do not telephone. E-mail submissions are welcome.

Richard Wilmarth, Owner
Dead Metaphor Press
303.939.0268 (Phone & FAX)
PO Box 2076
Boulder CO 80306-2076
wilmartr@colorado.edu

Booklist available upon request. Sample chapbooks are available for $6 postpaid.

Robert Brown
Melpomene and Thalia
719.564.3025
2113 Elmwood Ln.
Pueblo CO 81002

Not currently accepting manuscripts. List of titles available upon request.

PUBLISHERS (CONT.)

Catherine O'Neill Thorn, Owner
O'Neill Publishing
303.697.1317
303.697.9799 (FAX)
PO Box 53
Indian Hills CO 80454
ONeillPub@aol.com

Publishing, Editing & Writing:
Professional Quality • Personal Service • Reasonable Rates. Typesetting/Page Layout & Design, including word processing; Editing and Poetry Consultation; Free-lance writing: poetry, journalism, nonfiction.

10 percent discount to poets who mention this ad.

Tony Moffeit
Pueblo Poetry Project, Dept. PM
719.549.2751
719.549.2738 (FAX)
1501 E. 7th St.
Pueblo CO 81001
moffeit@uscolo.edu

Not considering manuscripts at present. Backlist, mostly out-of-print, chapbooks by Pueblo poets & anthologies of poets associated with the Pueblo Poetry Project.

Joel Scherzer
Quick Books
719.543.6858
PO Box 222
Pueblo CO 81002

Not currently accepting manuscripts. Back issues of poetry chapbooks and the literary magazine, ***Look Quick***, available. Send for list of publications.

Javana Richardson
StarsEnd Creations
303.694.1664
303.694.4098 (FAX)
8547 E. Arapahoe Rd. #J224
Greenwood Village CO 80112
jmr@starsend.com
Web Site: www.starsend.com

StarsEnd Creations, publishes both fiction and non-fiction. We work in the fiction genres, mystery, science fiction, soft horror, historical and some mainstream. Our non-fiction includes historical, poetry, cooking and some computer.

Kathleen Adams, LPC
The Center for Journal Therapy
PO Box 963
Arvada CO 80001
303.421.2298
303.421.1255 (FAX)
E-mail: KayAdams@aol.com
Author, JOURNAL TO THE SELF and THE WAY OF THE JOURNAL. Experienced, professional, dynamic speaker/workshop leader on any aspect of journal writing as a tool for growth and healing. Clinical trainings for helping professionals, ongoing therapeutic writing groups, summer intensives.

Lee Ballentine
Box 102650
Denver CO 80250
E-mail: leebal@sni.net
303.756.5222
Surrealist poet Lee Ballentine has published some 300 poems in *Abraxas, ACM, Caliban, Exquisite Corpse, Mississippi Mud, Portland Review,* and many other journals and anthologies, and in his four books of poems. His anthology POLY, which James Laughlin wrote was "pushing up into the Amazon of the new poetry," is an Anatomy of Wonder 'Best Book,' part of the core collection every library should hold. He's won awards for poetry and edited work, and has been a guest at the Willamette Writers Conference, Metropolitan State College, & University of Denver. Lee travels and reads his work frequently across the country, and is available to read his poetry, discuss poetry, publishing, and the state of the arts. Member of PEN West.

Taylor J. Berry
1200 Galapago, Apt. 208
Denver CO 80204
303.825.2088
Published in the *Community News* and the *Denver Voice.* Performance poetry with music; has performed at Toads in the Garden.

Poet: Beth Bassein
24 Stovel Circle
Colorado Spgs. CO 80916-4704

Kathleen Cain
6636 Fenton St.
Arvada CO 80003
303.424.2452
CainK@csn.net
Poet, author, contributing editor for *The Bloomsbury Review,* available for readings, workshops, lectures on Irish/Celtic myth and poetry; beginning writers; women's spirituality. Let's talk!

Jane Carpenter
303.756.1386
Watch for Jane Carpenter's book, ART NOUVEAU DREAMS, due out soon. Call to reserve a copy.

Jack Collom
Boulder
303.444.1886
Author of 13 books and a CD. Performances & poetry workshops for children & adults.

Mary Crow
970.482.9923
Poet Laureate of Colorado
Colorado State University • English Dept.
Ft. Collins CO 80523
Available for Workshops and Readings.

Karen D'Attilo
970.927.4949
PO Box 3177 • Nederland CO 80466
E-mail: 102201,1716@compuserve.com
Poems as gifts: your description of a topic or friend becomes a personal poem. Rates upon request.

poems sometimes
dance from my pencil

like I would, if I wasn't afraid

laughing and sailing
around the room
saying things
only safe

in thought or script

as I quietly hide
behind thin scratches
on a paper wall

"I write about things that touch, move, nurture, overwhelm, delight and challenge me to grow . . . Poetry is one of those rare creative things that help us to become what we know."

Patricia Dubrava
303.298.7063
E-mail: pat_keuning@cudenver.dps.edu
Poet, playwright, review and language arts teacher at Denver School of the Arts. Available for summer workshops.

Fred Ferraris
PO Box 65 • Lyons CO 80540
303.823.9362
Pubs.: Older Than Rain (Selva Editions, 1997); Marpa Point (Blackberry Books, 1976); *Boulder Planet; Phase & Cycle; Glassworks; Kuksu; Measure; Rocky Mountain Review,* others. Readings: w/ Jane Augustine, Clayton Eshleman, Rick Fields, Jackson Mac Low, Peter Orlovsky, others in New York, Los Angeles, San Francisco, Boulder.

John Fox
PO Box 60189 • Palo Alto CA 94306
E-mail: jfoxcpt@aol.com
Author of Finding What You Didn't Lose and Poetic Medicines. Poetry workshops occasionally held in Denver, call 303-421.2298 or write for national calendar.

Roseanna Frechette 303.837.8425
Poetry, Yoga and Dance *performance, consultation and classes.* Call for info. reg. ongoing programs & potential workshops for all populations. Offering integrative approach to creative process in a variety of settings, including classrooms. Specializing in programs for kids. Winner of Nat'l. Outstanding Program Award for "The Power of Poetic Voice" at Metro Denver's Girls Incorporated, 1997.

Art Goodtimes
Cloud Acre • Box 160
Norwood CO 81423
970.327.4775
goodtimes@infozone.org
Pubs.: Que Linda! (No Fat Mama & A/C Dick Press, 1993); Embracing the Earth (Homeward Press, 1994); *Upriver Downriver; Sun; Petroglyph; Poiesis; Wild Earth.*

Ed Hanson
7630 Leyden Lane
Commerce City CO 80022
303.287.9026 Home
303.438.4469 Work

Jana Hayes
c/o Janice Hayes
4835 Stanton Rd.
Co. Spgs. CO 80918
719.599.9633
Has published in various small magazines, including *the eleventh MUSE, Beloit Poetry Journal; Writer's Forum; Hamline Journal.* Books: New House: A Book of Women (San Marcos Press, 1972; rept. Sudden Jungle Press, 1982); The Hunger (Mellon Poetry Press, 1996); co-editor, Wingbone: Poetry from Colorado (Sudden Jungle Press, 1986).

Lois Hayna
403 Locust Drive
Colo. Spgs., CO 80907
719.599.0502
lhayna@kktv.com
Books: Never Trust a Crow (out of print), Book of Charms, Northern Gothic.

Laura Hershey
PO Box 9004 • Denver CO 80209
303.733.8717 (Phone)
303.733.9191 (fax)
E-mail: LauraHershey@CompuServe.com
Avail. for poetry readings at conferences, rallies, & other events. Hershey's poetry concerns human rights and personal empowerment. It has been well-received by a wide range of audiences

including feminists, peace activists, people with disabilities, college students, lesbians/gays, progressives, etc.

Woody Hildebrant
PO Box 4241
Grand Junction CO 81501-4241
970.255.8519

Poets of the Open Range • No Holds Bard Productions • HooDoo Rangers Performance Group
Investigative Poetry; Transcendental Metallurgy; Surrealistic Ecology. Hosts open stage for poetry every Tues. at 8 p.m. at The Station in Grand Junction. Avail. as a poet/performer for readings.

Anselm Hollo
c/o Writing & Poetics
The Naropa Institute
2130 Arapahoe Avenue
Boulder CO 80302

Most recent books: CORVUS (1995, Coffee House Press) and AHOE (1997, Smokeproof Press). Avail. for readings, occasional workshops, poetry & poetics panels.

Joseph Hutchison
PO Box 266
Indian Hills, CO 80454
Phone: 303.762.7550
FAX: 303.762.7909
E-mail: jgh@citylim.com

Joseph is the author of BED OF COALS (winner of the 1994 Colorado Poetry Award), HOUSE OF MIRRORS, the 1982 Colorado Governor's Award volume SHADOW-LIGHT, and several other collections. He has published in *American Poetry Review, Denver Quarterly, Hudson Review, Mississippi Review, Ohio Review, Poetry* (Chicago), and many anthologies. Born and raised in Denver, he teaches writing at the University of Denver's University College and co-owns City Limits Books, located near Teikyo-Loretto Heights College in SW Denver.

Full Scale, Inc.	Denver Office:
PO Box 266	3094 S. Federal Blvd.
Indian Hills CO 80454	Denver CO 80236

Mark Irwin
3875 S. Cherokee St.
Englewood CO 80110
303.762.6336

Pubs.: *The Atlantic, Kenyon Review, The Nation, Paris Review.* Author of five books. Avail. for readings & workshops.

Ron Jaeger
4117-D South Mobile Cr.
Aurora, CO 80013
303.699.9679
E-mail: Poiesis001@aol.com

Creator & instructor of the "Six Steps to Writing Poetry." Avail. for one-to-one, group, or classroom instruction.

Bruce Kauffman
303.722.9944

Denver area poet, has read primarily along the Front Range. Currently hosts a weekly poetry reading in Denver.

Marilyn Krysl
University of Colorado-Boulder
303.492.8944
krysl@spot.colorado.edu

Marilyn Krysl is the author of WARSCAPE WITH LOVERS, which won the Cleveland State Prize, 1996, six other books of poetry and two books of stories. She has served as Artist in Residence at the Center for Human Caring, worked for Peace Brigade International in Sri Lanka and at Mother Teresa's hospice in Calcutta. She directs the Writing Program at University of Colorado, Boulder.

Michelle Lampkin
2836 Vine St.
Denver CO 80205
303.297.9197

Author of the book SOCIETY AND THE SOCIAL WAR: A POET AT LARGE. Writer, conducts therapeutic poetry workshops, also available for readings.

Ira Liss
1302 Columbine, #204
Denver CO 80206-2347
303.377.4417
Ira Liss delights audiences with his humorous, conversational style. Versatile, he writes and performs original music, songs, monologues, poems, comedy and theater pieces. He can accompany himself on piano or keyboard, performs one-man shows, MCs, & also happily collaborates with others. He's avail. to lead writing & theater performance workshops. Currently, he performs regularly with the Open Rangers.

Brian T. McCauley
3889 E. 121st Ave.
Thornton CO 80241
303.254.9166
BMc121041@aol.com
Poet published in literary journals. Available for readings.

Sandra McNew
16 Valley Place #602
Co. Spgs. CO 80903
719.632.4374
Past president of Poetry West and editor of *the eleventh MUSE* literary mag. Winner of awards for poetry and short stories, and currently working on a novel that incorporates poetry.

Mary Jo Mauro
Pueblo
719.544.6089
Poetry and Performance Art.

Jennifer Maybury
Littleton CO
14-years-old, began writing poetry when she was 12. Her first book includes poems about adolescent feelings of love, fear, guilt, friendship, and many emotions of the present-day teenager. Take A Number, Poetry in E-Motion (ISBN 1-889120-08-1), paperback, $10.95, was released in April 1997. It is listed in the on-line catalog at http://www.starsend.com and is avail. from Ingram, Baker & Taylor and Bighorn Booksellers and in bookstores. Jennifer is an intelligent and inspiring performer and enjoys reading and speaking to the public. She can be reached via E-mail at jkm@starsend.com, by mail at StarsEnd Creations, 8547 E. Arapahoe Rd. #J224, Greenwood Village, CO 80112, or by phone at 303.694.1664.

Jim Merrill, Poet
5066 Buckingham Rd.
Boulder CO 80301
303.581.9433

Ann Miller
915 19th St.
Golden, Co. 80401
303.279.7373
Ann Miller has published poems in journals such as the *Hampden-Sydney Review, Poem, The Connecticut River Review* and *Ellipsis.* She is co-director of Poetry & More, a coffee house reading forum.

Tony Moffeit
719.584.3401
719.549.2751
Blues, beat and jazz poet. NEA recipient. Jack Kerouac Award recipient. Thomas Hornsby Ferril Award recipient. Poet-in-Residence, University of Southern Colo. Performances/Workshops: $150; with guitarist or saxophonist: $250.

Open Rangers
Contact SETH
303.458.7952
Working the Open Range of creative expression by showcasing innovative ways of presenting poetry for stage, audio cassette and video. Always searching for new talent and creative collaboration. See "Random Axe of Rhyme," listed in the Events section of this Guide.

Veronica Patterson
2425 Agate Drive
Loveland CO 80538
970.669.7010.
Books: How to Make a Terrarium (Cleveland State University), The Bones Remember: A Dialogue (Stone Graphics Press). Ucross Foundation residency; recipient 1997-98 Creative Writing Fellowship (CCA); first prize 1997 Amherst Peregrine poetry contest; first prize 1997 Salt Hill Journal poetry contest. Publications include *Southern Poetry Review, Louisville Review, Georgia Review* (essay), *Colorado Review, The Bloomsbury Review,* others.

Carson Reed
303.296.2654
Lodo1@aol.com
Carson Reed is the Author of Tie Up the Strong Man (Bread & Butter Press) and three other books of poetry. His poetry has been published in journals such as *Real-Poetik, Yellow Silk, The Sun, Artisan, Bizara, Harp, Meshuggah, Stick, BYOD, Rant,* and *The New Censorship* and has been anthologized in several books. He has led poetry, creative writing, publishing workshops at K-12 schools throughout the Front Range. He is also a writing mentor for America OnLine.

Vicki Rottman
Writer/Artist
The Coffee Break Book
303.831.8661

Renée Ruderman
1250 Humboldt #903
Denver, CO 80218
303.556.8447
Poetry & Creative Writing Instructor at MSCD. Author of Poems from the Rooms Below (Permanence Press, 1995), ISBN 0-938075-58-6. Available for readings and workshops.

Jacqueline (Jackie) St. Joan
1339 Quince St.
Denver CO 80220
303.355.0504

Joy Sawyer
303.643.1885
Performance poet. Available for poetry readings, workshops, church services. M.A., NYU. *Mars Hill Review* poetry editor and *Inklings* columnist.

Tim Van Schmidt
970.493.3113

Good and Hard

That's how it's been
climbing up the golden current.
It sleekens the soul,
time shooting past
so fast, you haven't
got time enough to swim.

Imagine Pablo Neruda performing with John Cage: **TVS & two fingers** mix poetry with "sound art," played on homemade and found instruments. Now performing 20-90 minute shows on the Front Range.

Clay Schonberger
303.986.7043
Author of nine editions of *Molten Treads*, collections of poetry, essays, short stories, and drawings. Experienced reader of his own poetry, actor, musician, painter, with a BA in Fine Art. Currently working on *MT-10*: a collection of the previous works, and a novel, The Transformation of Thondar.

Gary Schroeder
Wild Wind Ranch
1429 N. Castlewood Dr.
Franktown CO 80116-9015
Tel: 303.660.6029
E-Mail: schroederpoetbudo@msn.com
Books: THE SLENDER NAME, MISTAKEN LIGHTS, ADJACENT SOLITUDES, A SONG FOR OCCUPATIONS (ed.). Member: Colorado Authors League. Available for readings and workshops.

February
A warm day in winter,
Wasps buzzing at the west wall.
All day long
A busy mind.

Jerry Smaldone: Poet
6305 Newland St.
Arvada CO 80003

Steven Smith
Poet/Performing Artist
PO Box 6270
Cheyenne WY 82003
307.635.2359
Authentic West Coast beat poetry... Stir-fried Southern accent... Blended and seasoned with Western flavor... Side order of live theater... Served to perfection.

Leonard P. Streifel
2332 S. Jasmine Pl.
Denver, CO 80222
303.758.0322
I am available to write poetry or lyrics for individuals and organizations. I also am interested in working with music composers.

Constance Studer
303.665.3818
Available for poetry readings, workshops, master classes. M.A. in Creative Writing. Registered Nurse. Much of my work deals with medical issues from different viewpoints. Books: PRAYER TO A PURPLE GOD (Mellen U. Poetry Press, 1996.)

Catherine O'Neill Thorn
PO Box 53
Indian Hill CO 80454
303.697.1317
303.697.9799 (fax)
E-mail: ONeillPub@aol.com
Published poet, journalist and author of TRISKELION; served as the Colorado Council on the Arts coordinator for Tumble-Words; poetry judge for the Colorado Book Award; has performed at numerous venues throughout the state and published in national literary journals as well as local publications.

Rawdon Tomlinson
2020 S. Grant
Denver CO 80210
303.733.6736
Widely published. 1996 Colorado Book Award for DEEP RED (University Press of Florida). 27 years experience readings and workshops.

Gail Waldstein, M.D.
Poet/Writer
1235 Vine St.
Denver CO 80206
303.321.1137

Bob Wearden
719.578.9332
If you should need
Words to excite . . .
Have poems to read,
Poems to recite.

Book: MY PEN RAN WILD

Richard Wilmarth
303.939.0268
Richard Wilmarth's poetry is emotional, comical, tragical, accessible, entertaining.

Terrence (TC) Wright
Denver
303.863.7147
www.poets.com/terrencecwright.html
Experienced poet seeks opportunities to read his original poetry.